What Made America Great
Secrets Removed from History

By Jim MacDonald

Edited by David McLaughlin
1st Revision

Printed by CreateSpace – Kindle Direct publishing - Amazon
Printed in the United States of America
What Made America Great: Secrets Removed from History

Cover designed by:
Jim MacDonald with Kindle Cover Design

All Photographs were taken by:
Jim MacDonald

FIRST REVISION 2019

I've dedicated this book to my Lord and Savior Jesus Christ who inspired the writing of this book to reach America, reminding her: He is still in control. He created this great nation for His purposes and is searching for leaders who are willing to step up and say— "Here am I. Send me!"

What Made America Great

Chapter 17

Preface

This book was written as a starting point for America to begin her journey back to American Exceptionalism. For more than twenty years I've studied the Declaration of Independence and the Constitution of the United States while teaching friends and family the "secret" history of our founding—things that were removed from our school textbooks starting just over a hundred years ago. Hearing them ask (like I did), why they hadn't heard of these things before—and want to hear more.

The founding of this Great Nation was NO simple task and repairing it won't be simple either. But we're beyond the point of waiting and hoping things fix themselves. When Ben Franklin was asked what type of government the Founders had given us. He answered, "a republic if you can keep it." Our country is declining at a rapid pace. If we don't return to the foundation that made this nation exceptional, we risk losing the nation we know and love. If America falls from its pedestal, the world will not have a nation to look up to. Countries like England, France or Spain could argue there isn't much difference between them and us and they'd be right. America has abandoned the principles that made her exceptional. Today we're only exceptional in the hearts and minds of those Americans who have yet to forget our founding principles. We must equip people with this forgotten knowledge so America can rediscover her former glory and get back to leading from the front.

Today kids strive to be like Lebron James of the LA Lakers or Tom Brady of the New England Patriots. Or perhaps, Steve Jobs of Apple or even the President of the United States. People dream of being better than they are, of achieving more than they've accomplished, and we look to others who've gone before us as examples. Nations aren't any different. Since the founding of this country, many have followed our lead and developed their form of government based on the bar set by America. Unfortunately, many of our leaders today no longer want America to be that shining city set upon a hill. They desire for our country to be average like the rest of the nations of the world, so they've worked to undermine us. Since 'We the People' still hunger for exceptionalism, America is inadequate to participate in the One World Order...which is the 'ultimate goal' for many of America's elites[1].

I look forward to the day when our children and grandchildren come home from school and ask if we knew our Founders believed God, prayer and the Holy Bible were vitally important to education in school and to the success of America.

The material in this book is a conglomeration of numerous courses, many seminars and countless books I've read. What makes it unique is the vast array of material narrowed down to around three hundred manageable pages. The material omitted is still extremely important, and I highly recommend you research it. Unfortunately, people don't have the time or desire to invest in the research necessary. Please consider this as your 'Beginner's Guide to Rediscovering America.'

This book reveals how following God's principles led to the rise of America—ignoring them led to the downward slide—and how following them again will return us to greatness. I hope God's inspiration leads you to seek the truth and spread this information to others who you have some influence over. Teach your children and grandchildren—teach your peers so they will, in turn, teach their children and grandchildren.

It's critically important we know and understand:

- Who our Founders were
- What the Constitution is about
- And the influence God played in America.

How can I be so certain of this? –Because the current and past leaders of the progressive movement have worked zealously hard to remove God and the Constitution from the classroom and the public square. They know America can't be transformed if our children are taught and understand God and the Constitution. A powerful case will be made for this as we move along.

The Founders believed the success of America depended on every child knowing and understanding the Holy Bible and the Constitution of the United States. We must fight tooth and nail to

---

[1] Reference United Nation's "Agenda 21" and "Agenda 2030"

restore these Godly principles into every classroom. It's a battle against the progressive ideology—and America CAN'T afford to lose this fight.

I'm a God-fearing, Bible-believing Christian man. Like countless others, I've been praying for America—for many years now. I became interested in studying the Declaration of Independence and the Constitution when I kept hearing people talk about this 'separation of church and state'—how God isn't allowed in our schools and government buildings. This common misconception troubled me so much I set out to find the truth. The more I learned, the more I realized how little I knew about the founding of America—and that frustrated me. I wondered why so much time was wasted on trivial things in school when the true founding of this nation was hardly discussed.

Assuming I skipped school on the days the teachers discussed these events, I shared the material with my four adult children—and found their knowledge was limited as well. In fact, most people are as uneducated as I was. Many people I spoke with either lacked the desire to learn or kept asking additional questions. Suddenly, I became the 'expert' in their eyes. Which inspired me to continue to learn and teach more. While praying for our nation, I felt at some point God would call me to teach this in a more official setting. However, one night He woke me up early with thoughts about writing this book. At first, I tried to ignore it and go back to sleep. Five hours later, I was sitting in my living room finishing the outline. At 6:30 in the morning I thanked God I didn't have to work that day…and went back to bed.

My prayer for you is this: That the knowledge you receive from this book will inspire you:

- To become more educated in the truth of America
- Understand the importance of being politically educated
- Be a well-informed voter
- Become politically active
- And know God is in control.

May God Bless You and May God Bless America.

Jim MacDonald

Acknowledgment

The Declaration of Independence and the Constitution of the United States were written by true statesmen who were inspired by God Himself. These two documents work collectively together—and condensing this vast array of information into a simple, informative, concise and accurate way, is nearly impossible. Numerous books have been written on every topic covered here—and I'd be remiss if I didn't acknowledge the scholars who've spent their lives researching and studying these documents and the men who wrote them. So, let me give credit where credit is due.

Starting with Hillsdale College's free online courses: visit www.hillsdale.edu and take the following courses: Constitution 101, Constitution 201, The Presidency and the Constitution and The U.S. Supreme Court. Also, they've written a book called "The U.S. Constitution." This book is filled with letters, speeches, and documents that will assist in your research into the fascinating history of America.

Next, are seminars and videos from a patriot named Rick Green. I've seen Mr. Green speak several times over the years and have purchased and studied much of his material. After reading this book, I hope you will visit his website www.RickGreen.com and purchase one of my favorite CD-based training programs called "Constitution Alive." In this program, the Green family takes you deep into a fun, entertaining and very informative study of these founding documents right in Liberty Hall. There's no better investment for you and your family.

David Barton's website www.wallbuilders.com. David has spent a lifetime studying, researching and teaching America about our founding. His passion and commitment to the truth of our history are second to none. I also recommend reading a book he wrote called: Original Intent.

Next, is a book called "The Heritage Guide to the Constitution" from the Heritage Foundation. Their online website www.heritage.org and the information you will receive from them is phenomenal.

My favorite book is by William J. Federer called America's God and Country. It's over 700 pages of quotes about God and America—from the school system, Supreme Court decisions, Founding Fathers to modern day Presidents. Every time I open this book, I'm fascinated with the stories and quotes I read.

Two other books I recommend are "Vindicating the Founders" by Thomas G. West and "The Five Thousand Year Leap" by W. Cleon Skousen. Terrific Books!!!

The final acknowledgments go to several of our Founders. Most of the definitions called out in this book come directly from the original dictionary call: The American Dictionary of the English Language by Noah Webster 1828. Also, Signet Classics put two important books together called: The Federalist Papers and the Anti-Federalist Papers—Great resources.

Most of the materials shared were derived from the above resources — over ten thousand pages of fantastic material. The nuggets provided in the book are your beginner's guide to our founding — basic information to get you started on your journey to help us rehabilitate America.

So, let's begin...

Chapter 1

What's This Journey About?

America was built on the foundation of God. He set aside a beautiful piece of property for His people to build their home and spread the Good News of our Lord and Savior Jesus Christ. God began by placing pieces of the American puzzle together beginning when Christopher Columbus discovered the new land (acknowledging there are other theories).

When the foundation of God stands firm, we enjoy natural laws, natural rights, absolute truth, and the ability to raise virtuous children. This allows us to experience freedom and liberty, own property and pursue happiness.

In 1776, it was time for America to break away from England to chart its destiny. Of course, this came with huge fanfare and major discouragement from the King. Thomas Jefferson, one of our Founding Fathers, penned the words of the Declaration of Independence in 17 days and submitted them to Congress for review on June 28, 1776. On July 2, the document was edited and unanimously voted for on July 4, 1776. America was on her own— led by true statesmen like George Washington, Thomas Jefferson, John Adams, and countless others.

These statesmen helped America write a mission statement and an owner's manual. They called these documents, the Declaration of Independence and the Constitution of the United States. The Declaration of Independence eloquently describes who America is and what she stands for. The Constitution of the United States sets the boundaries and guidelines for the operation of this great land God provided for us.

The Declaration of Independence states that: ALL men (meaning men and women of all races) are created equal by God.

And God gave us rights which CANNOT be taken away. Among these rights are:

- Life—the ability to choose how we live our lives providing we aren't encroaching on someone else's chosen way of life.
- Liberty—being FREE from oppressive restrictions imposed by an authority that tries to regulate America's life against her own moral and virtuous beliefs.
- The pursuit of Happiness—which means to affirm that "religion, morality, and knowledge are essential to the happiness of mankind."

The Constitution was written as guidelines for our leaders to follow. These guidelines state the elected officials (our federal government) shall protect our rights from ALL powers both foreign and domestic that attempt to take away our God-given rights. The federal government's authority is authorized by the people in whom they govern.

Yet many Americans have little if any knowledge or understanding of these documents which is at the heart of America's problems (problems we'll discuss as we move forward). The first Chief Justice of the U.S. Supreme Court said this about our Constitution: "Every member of the State (speaking of each American citizen) ought diligently to read and to study the Constitution, of his country, and teach the rising generation to be free. By knowing their rights, they will sooner perceive when they are violated, and be the better prepared to defend and assert them."[2]

In reading this book, you'll gain a strong understanding of "What Made America Great." This knowledge will include:

- What's in our Declaration of Independence and Constitution—and why it's important to follow.
- Where the Progressive Movement originated from and why it must be destroyed.
- What is Socialism and how destructive the philosophy is for the American way of life.

---

[2] John Jay, Correspondence (N. Y., 1890), I. 160-161, 163-164 passim. 2

- What the Administrative State is and how it has usurped much of our freedom
- What are natural laws and natural rights—and the impact they have on our lives.
- What's absolute truth and why it's important.
- Why all decisions from the Supreme Court MUST be based on "original intent."

More importantly, you will learn that America was built on the foundation of God. Each section in this book will be brief and to the point. Plus, there's a fifty-question quiz at the end to test your aptitude.

The Constitution cleverly divides the federal government into three major groups: The Presidency, Congress and the Judiciary. The purpose of this division is to keep any one group from becoming too powerful. The Founders believed that by splitting the power into three groups, no one group would allow another group to take any of their power away. Unfortunately, the Founders were incorrect on this assumption. Congress and the states have allowed both the President and the judicial system to usurp much of the power given to them—but I digress.

The Constitution was written to LIMIT the powers of the federal government. It identifies exactly what the three branches of government are allowed and not allowed to do. ALL other responsibilities, not stated in the Constitution, are to be addressed by the states. The Founders authorized the federal government JUST enough power to perform the duties set by the Constitution and no more—the sovereign states maintained the remainder of the power. The Founders believed the PEOPLE would have more control over state governments than they would over the federal government.

The President

The President's number one duty as the Executive of America is to protect all the American people. Next is to enforce all laws written by Congress whether he agrees with them or not. He is:

- Elected by the citizens of the United States to serve a 4-year term with the ability to be re-elected for a second term.
- He is the Commander in Chief of the United States Military
- He is given the power to veto bills that come to his desk if he feels they are not in the best interest of the people.

The Congress

Congress is given the authority to write ALL laws that govern our land. Neither the President nor the Judiciary has this authority. Congress is divided into two separate groups, the House of Representatives and the Senate. Each House has separate but similar responsibilities. The following is a combined summary of many of their duties.

- House of Representatives (the larger house – 435 members) are elected for two years and can be re-elected for additional terms with no term limits.
- The Senate (the smaller house – 100 members – 2 from each state) is elected to 6 years with the ability to be re-elected for additional terms with no term limits.
- Congress has the power to structure the court system.
- Congress has the sole power to impeach and try any executive for wrongdoing.
- Congress shall make all laws that govern our land.
- Any money spent by the federal government must first be authorized by Congress.

The Judiciary

The highest court in the land is the Supreme Court. Congress may set up inferior courts to lessen the burden of the Supreme Court. Their powers extend to all cases, in law and equity, arising under the Constitution, the laws of the United States and Treaties made.

- The President appoints the Justices, and the Senate confirms them.
- They may hold office for a time of good behavior, with no limitation of time.

■ They are to rule based on the original intent of the Constitution, not political intent.

The Constitution continues to state many of the laws and procedures the federal government may perform and what it may not perform. It's clear that ANYTHING not so stated in this document is to be handled by the sovereign states. If the Constitution does not spell out a duty or responsibility assigned to the above branches, then they are automatically assigned to the individual states, period.

Now in the late 1800s, early 1900s a well-organized movement began to guide America in a different direction. Despite all the miracles and wisdom which the Founders experienced and wrote about, this movement rejected the Founder's philosophy of government and their God—laying the groundwork for the progressive movement that will be discussed later.

Fast Forward to Today

The initiatives of the progressive movement have allowed the federal government to usurp (steal) powers they were not entitled to from other branches and states. Ironically, these states and branches of government did little to resist the takeover of their power.

One example of the progressive's initiatives was to spread what's become a common belief stating we should have "a separation of church and state." This is a myth that's spread and taken legs throughout our political system, media, and schools. There's no mention of a separation of church and state in the Declaration of Independence or the Constitution. But you will find something similar in the constitution of the USSR or United Soviet Socialist Republic (Russia). It goes like this: "The Constitution of the United Soviet Socialist Republic from 1922 till 1991 stated the following: Article 124: In order to ensure to citizens freedom of conscience, the church in the U.S.S.R. is separated from the State and the school from the church."[3] Many of the early progressives studied in Russia and Germany. They learned this teaching and have worked hard to incorporate it into our educational system ever since. You don't have to look far to discover they've succeeded.

Another tenant of the progressive initiatives was to discredit the Founders. For example, George Washington was by far a man of wisdom and faith. He was a strong and courageous Commander-in-Chief. But, what's taught in school is that Washington chopped down a cherry tree—of which there's no evidence. The story originated from a book store owner by the name of Parson Weems in 1809 who wrote this tale in a book called George Washington the Great. With everything known about George, there's little known about his childhood including a cherry tree incident. Our Founders lived remarkable lives that could've been shared in school, so why was this story so prevalent? We'll discuss a few of their stories in chapter 4.

Another effort to discredit the Founders states they were racist, and the Constitution was about keeping the black man in slavery. While many of the Founders did own slaves, nearly sixty percent of them were the original abolitionist. They formed a movement to end the African and Indian slave trade. They believed slavery needed to end for America to grow strong and prosperous. And to truly unite as one nation under God. Slavery will be discussed in chapter 7—but understand this, the body of the Constitution put in place many factors designed to end slavery, not to keep it flourishing. The byproduct of the Founder's efforts was that institutional slavery not only ended in America but around the world as well.

In the closing chapter, we'll chart the course for repairing this nation. Currently, America has an overwhelming national debt, and a policy of corruption in Washington, D.C. Unfortunately, the people believe it's just part of the beast we call government. Terrorism, both domestic and abroad will play a significant role in every American's life if we don't figure out how to end it. Crime rate, abortion rate, and the drug abuse rate are at all-time highs. For the first time in American history, we have

---

[3] Constitution of the United Soviet Socialist Republic. Article 124. Gary Demar, God and Government (Atlanta: American Vision Press, 1982), p. 163. David Barton, The Myth of Separation (Aledo, TX: WallBuilder Press, 1991), p.45

more entrepreneurs closing their businesses than we have new businesses starting up. Let's just say we have a lot of work to do.

America is running at a rate that's barely manageable, let alone recognizable. Many of our leaders have bypassed the Constitution as if it never existed. They're running with a mission that would make Lenin, Mussolini, and Hitler proud. Today we're at a point where they're not even trying to hide their motives. The American people are deceptively informed of their mission. They've baited people with free phones, free health care, and free college education without telling them the payment for this erodes our precious freedom. America is falling head over heels for this because they don't understand what "freedom" really means. It's difficult to start up a new business—as new regulations shut down businesses every day. Regardless of the political party, our elected officials have joined in on this assault against our freedom. The wisdom of our Founders such as George Washington warned the country against "faction" or political parties because he believed it would divide the nation—clearly, he was right.

Add the media and their political agenda; you can see why we have a mess on our hands. Look at the abuse any political leader must put themselves and their family through in order to serve our country in a political office. Is there any wonder why few men and women with high moral character and integrity run for office? This is a shame, and it needs to stop.

After discussing the challenges above, let's look at what America has going for her. We have the greatest military in the history of the world—for protecting our way of life. This military enlists and trains the bravest, wisest, most loyal people in the world—combined with the greatest technology the world has ever seen. Second is our charitable hearts. No nation in the world gives more than we do. If there's a need in our own country or around the world, "We the People" will rise to the occasion and contribute to the cause. Regardless of whether it's a natural disaster or a man-made disaster, we rise and contribute both time and money. Thirdly, since we're a free nation, innovation in this country is second to none. No country has contributed more to improving the lives of people in America or around the world. Lastly, Americans have resolved. When the chips are down, and there doesn't seem to be a way out. When the fight gets tough, and we're not sure we can make it. Americans will rise to the occasion against all the odds and win the battle.

Are you tired of the status quo but are not sure anything can be done to fix it? Every person wants a better lifestyle, but many are living lives of quiet desperation. Now granted, it doesn't look like it can be fixed. The progressives, who set out to change America, have moved the needle to where we are today. We must stop this "progress" and reverse the trends back to the original intent of the Constitution. It took a hundred and thirty years to get where we are today, and it may take that long to get back—but we must get started. My hope is you feel the same way and want to know how to go about it. If we do our part to make the corrections necessary, God will intercede and heal our land quicker than it took to destroy it.

It's our job to hold the politicians and the media accountable for reporting the facts rather than forcing their agenda on us with fake news stories. It's our job to elect virtuous politicians and judges while not allowing business leaders and educators to influence us falsely. Jefferson wrote the following:

> *"If a nation expects to be ignorant and free, in a state of civilization, it expects what never was and never will be."*[4]
> *"No other sure foundation can be devised for the preservation of freedom and happiness...Preach... and crusade against ignorance: establish and improve the law for educating the common people. Let our countrymen know that the people alone can protect us against these evils"*[5] (speaking of our misguided government).

Our country's counting on us to get involved. We can't sit around and say "well, there's nothing I can do. These politicians are a bunch of liars, and my vote doesn't mean anything anyway." If millions of people start searching for the truth, share what they've learned and encourage others to do the same—what an impact that would make on America. We'll come out of this

---

[4] *The Writings of Thomas Jefferson*. Edited by Paul Leicester Ford 10 vols. New York: G.P. Putnam's Sons, 1892-99 vol. 4

[5] *The Writings of Thomas Jefferson*. Edited by Albert Ellery Bergh. 20 vols. Washington: The Thomas Jefferson Memorial Association, 1907, 5:396-397

stronger, leaner and meaner. Don't forget what social media can do with the truth. Your opinions and votes are very important. Make it an educated and informed opinion. Your children, grandchildren, America and the rest of the world are counting on us to make informed and accurate decisions. It's not too late yet, but soon, it will be.

Let's combine our American qualities with the plan at the end of this book—we'll have a growing, thriving, morally straight country that's a beacon on the hill once again. I believe in America. I believe in you. Let's change one person at a time by teaching them the principles you learn here. With God's help, we CAN repair the foundation of America.

Washington Monument, Washington, D.C.

Chapter 2

Your State as a Sovereign Country

What if America had been divided into 50 countries instead of states—and you lived in one of those countries? The governor of your state would be the President of your country. Each state would have the number of Senators and House of Representatives the state designates through their state constitution. The Supreme Court and inferior court Judges may be elected officials as well. Each country would draw its own constitution which would govern the land.

For example, Ohio has just over 11.5 million people. There's one governor, thirty-three Senators, ninety-nine House of Representatives (HR) and countless judges. On average it works out to be about one HR per 117,000 people and one Senator per 350,000 people. That's a lot of people for one person to represent. And since Ohio would be a sovereign country, we can pass an amendment to change the number as we so choose.

See how much more control or access you'd have to your representatives under this scenario as opposed to what we have in Washington D.C.? You'd have much more influence to impact the policy-making of your country. Now, how much easier would it be to rally a bunch of people together to make an impact on your politicians?

Looking at current social issues—if your country desired marriage to be between one man and one woman then pass a law stating so. On the other hand, if your country were for LGBTQ marriage, then you'd work with your politicians and pass a law favoring that. Take any other contentious issues of today such as abortion, gun control, welfare, etc. Your country could pass a law in whatever direction the people of your country wanted.

How about taxes? Today we pay federal, state and local income tax along with a Social Security and Medicare tax. We pay a sales tax, property tax, gas tax, sin tax, hotel tax just to name the obvious ones. If you add them up, it will run anywhere from thirty to sixty percent or more based on your income. Because we'd have more access to the ear of our politicians, we can certainly make sure they're pinching every penny possible. Our current tax rate would likely to be substantially lower. When a social program is presented, we'd look at the cost and decide whether we need that program or not. Does the country want to pay the extra tax to fund this program or not?

When the government taxes less, people keep more of their money. With more money in your pocket and less wasted on bloated, inefficient programs or special interest groups, you can give more to your church and any other special charity that pulls on your heartstrings. Think how much more impact the church or charity can make on the people's needs in your country. Think how much more efficient your country would run if the people are involved in the oversight of the government.

If each of the fifty countries made decisions based on what's in the best interest of their citizens—and you as a citizen of a neighboring country looked at their country and decided you wanted to move because you preferred their social, political and/or fiscal status better. You can make that decision. This essentially would create competition in each country in order to attract more people and companies from other countries — free enterprise, alive and well.

Now let's carry this concept a step further and add a centralized government—called the federal government. Since our countries are running smoothly, we don't want this federal government to become too powerful. We'll limit its power to a few designated items, so the individual countries of this continent can operate freely without worrying about outside interferences. We will give them control of things like our military, foreign affairs, interstate roads, interstate commerce, and printing of common a currency. They can make and monitor patents and copyrights to protect people's writings and inventions. We'll allow them to judge major disputes between the different countries. We'll call each of these countries states instead and call the continent The United States of America. Every state will send two Senators and a certain number of Representatives base on the population of their state to a ten-mile square piece of property we'll call Washington D.C. These representatives will be men and women of high moral standards and character. They'll be the best people the state has to offer. We'll have all fifty states ratify a very limiting document listing all the powers of this federal government and call it the Constitution of the United States. This federal government will assume no other powers except what is listed on the document.

This scenario is what the Founders envisioned when they established America over 230 years ago. They intended control to belong to the people and not politicians and bureaucrats in Washington D.C. They established the states to maintain most of the control.

Added Adversity to the Founders' Vision

While establishing their vision, the Founders faced a war with the greatest army and navy in the world, The British Empire. The king of this empire had no desire of releasing the land without a fight. Tensions were building for several years between Britain and the United States Colonies. The Boston Tea Party had erupted on December 16, 1773, causing problems over taxes imposed by the king. Soldiers were entering homes with what was called a general warrant to see if they were paying their fair share of taxes. During a standoff in Concord Massachusetts, on April 18, 1775, a "shot that was heard around the world" was fired. To this day, no one knows which side fired first, but the Revolutionary War had begun.

A year passed, and a group of leaders from all thirteen American colonies gathered to address the grievances each colony had against the King of England. If there were no way to resolve the conflict, they would have to do the unthinkable and declare independence. They clearly understood it would mean certain death to them and a loss of all their fortunes.

The decision was made to move forward. Thomas Jefferson wrote the Declaration of Independence and 56 men from all 13 states signed their names to the document and submitted it to the king. The United States military were primarily farmers, rancher, blacksmiths, and craftsman. Some had received experience fighting alongside the British soldiers during the French and Indian war.

In January of 1776, there was a young man named Thomas Paine, who'd written and published a pamphlet called "Common Sense" which made a passionate case for liberty over the monarchy. This pamphlet had over a half a million copies in print with only three million people in the country. Fortunately, it inspired many Americans to join in on the fight for freedom. What kind of odds would Vegas give the Americans back in 1776 to win the war against Great Britain? Without Divine Providence, the American's had no hope for victory. The Founders wrote numerous stories of Divine intervention which will be shared in chapter 4.

What Altered the Course of the World?

Whether you believe in the world view of evolution and the earth is millions of years old, or you believe in the biblical world view and the earth is over six thousand years old—ask yourself this question. What phenomenon occurred three hundred plus years ago that had not happened the previous five thousand plus years earlier or tens of millions of years earlier? In other words, what switch got flipped to create all the innovations, medicines, high technology, methods of transportation that's been developed over the last three hundred years that didn't occur say one or two thousand years earlier. Why has the world changed so much since America was discovered? Or five hundred years ago, in 1492 when Christopher Columbus discovered the new land? Why didn't these changes occur earlier? What held the world back during the previous fifty-five hundred years or the previous million years?

The answer is obvious but politically incorrect. It's called American Exceptionalism. What does that mean? It means for the first time in the history of the world; the people experienced pure, unadulterated freedom. For the first time, we did not have a ruler making most of our decisions. We could dream, create and invent. Our ideas were protected so we could benefit from our creations. We could be as successful as we desired to be. Americans could own businesses and property. We could fail as often as necessary. When we failed, we could get back up and try again. We could give glory to our Creator without offending a king. We could worship as we choose. We lived in a nation where the people are protected from enemies, both foreign and domestic. A land where our borders are protected by what is arguably the greatest military ever assembled—patriotic men and women who love our flag and all that it stands for. People who will not back down when the fight gets tough.

Although modern-day consensus says we are not a country built on Judeo-Christian principles, our Founding Fathers would beg to differ. Their writings acknowledge story after story of God intervening in the issues of their day. We have a God that guides our steps. A God that helped the Founders develop a limited government where the people answer to God and the government answers to the people. This allows us to think, to create, to fail, to succeed, to improve and even start over if necessary. We have a heart for helping others. To make other people's lives better, to solve problems and establish any desired lifestyle we're willing to work for. We are Americans.

Our Founders knew full well that power corrupts. And by giving a group of people (in Washington D.C.) virtually unlimited power and money to do as they see fit with little accountability, we have the modern day "D.C. Swamp." For example:

- Congress has a tax-payer funded "slush fund" to pay off accusers who raise misconduct issues such as sexual harassment charges against Congressmen.[6]
- They spent over $100,000,000 for a harbor and an airport in a town with no roads and 75 full-time residents.[7]
- Congress spends millions of dollars on dead people who are still receiving food stamps plus 1000's of people receiving duplicate benefits, reference in the same report as above.
- $20,000,000 to remake "Sesame Street" for Pakistan.

These are just a few of the trillions of dollars the federal government wasted and continues to waste year after year. We

---

[6]   https://www.usatoday.com/story/opinion/2017/11/27/sexual-harassment-fund-exposes-congress-editorials-debates/898008001/
[7]   https://posey.house.gov/wasteful-spending/

must put an end to this. What if we divided this spending by 50 and gave the money back to the states, how much better would each state be? How much better off would you be if the government hadn't taken the cash from you, to begin with?

You don't have to look far to see how out of control federal government spending is. The federal government should not have this much control over the lives of the people. A large centralized government is what gives special interest groups so much control. Think how difficult it would be for a special interest group like the Abortion Lobby or the NRA Lobby to influence American policy if they had to reach out to all 50 state governments' elected officials separately? Power and control must be given back to the states where it belongs.

Chapter 3

Progressivism

The word progressivism or progressive party is not in Noah Webster's 1828 dictionary because the movement didn't exist at that time. Utilizing Random House Dictionary, it states:

- Progressivism means: the doctrines and beliefs of a progressive party.
- Progressive party means: 1. A party formed in 1912 under the leadership of Theodore Roosevelt, advocating popular control of the government, direct primaries, woman suffrage, etc. 2. A similar party formed in 1924 under the leadership of Robert M. La Follette. 3. A left-wing political party formed in 1948 under the leadership of Henry A. Wallace[8].

During the late 1800s, early 1900s a new philosophy came on the American scene. One that virtually rejected everything the Founders believed and experienced. They called this philosophy—progressivism. The premise behind this philosophy was built on science. Woodrow Wilson wrote:

> *"All that progressives ask, or desire is permission—in an era when development, evolution, is a scientific word—to interpret the Constitution according to the Darwinian principle; all they ask is recognition of the fact that a nation is a living thing and not a machine."*[9]

---

[8] The Random House Dictionary. (1985). New York, NY: Penguin Random House.
[9] The U.S. Constitution: a reader. (2012). Hillsdale, MI: Hillsdale College Press.p,641

Progressivism rejects the notion that the God of the universe exists and interacts in the affairs of man. Some may believe a higher power existed to start the ball rolling but has no further role. Darwinism is their "science" which justifies the philosophy that people and governments evolve. Therefore, the Constitution needs to evolve as well.

Since God doesn't exist in their world view, they can reject the notion that man was born free. John Dewey, an American philosopher, and psychologist wrote that freedom is not:

"something that individuals have as a ready-made possession." It's "something to be achieved." Freedom comes from the government and not from God. Which means there are no "natural rights or natural laws." Dewey wrote: "Natural rights and natural liberties exist only in the kingdom of mythological social zoology."[10]

The Founders believed God created man and gave us the gift of freedom and liberty and established a government to protect our freedom. Progressives believe people evolved with no real inherent value and governments are established to give us our freedom.

The preamble of the Massachusetts Constitution of 1780, written by John Adams states: "The body-politic is formed by a voluntary association of individuals: It is a social compact, by all shall be governed by certain laws for the common good."[11] The purpose of government, then, is to enforce the natural law for the citizens of the political community by securing the people's natural rights. The government is to secure freedom and liberty, not from poverty and welfare but from the despotic and predatory domination of some human beings over others.

Progressives see it differently. Dewey writes: *"the state has the responsibility for creating institutions under which individuals can effectively realize the potentialities that are theirs."* So, although "it is true that social arrangements, laws, institutions are

---

[10] Dewey, J., & Boydston, J. A. (2008). The later works of John Dewey, 1925-1953. Carbondale: Southern Illinois University Press.

[11] A Constitution or frame of government: agreed upon by the delegates of the people of the state of Massachusetts-Bay, in convention, begun and held at Cambridge, on the first of September 1779, and continued by adjournments, to the second of March 1780. (1784). Boston: Commonwealth of Massachusetts: Printed by Benjamin Edes & Sons, in Cornhill.

made for man, rather than that man is made for them," these laws and institutions "are not means for obtaining something for individuals, not even happiness. They are means of creating individuals... Individuality in a social and moral sense is something to be wrought out."[12] Progressives believe the government is responsible for creating individuals instead of protecting them and letting them create themselves.

The Progressives disagreed with the social compact idea Adams spoke of. Charles Merriam, a leading progressive political scientist, wrote: The individualistic ideas of the "natural right" school of political theory, endorsed in the Revolution, are discredited and repudiated... The origin of the state is regarded, not as the result of a deliberate agreement among men, but as the result of historical development, instinctive rather than conscious; and rights are considered to have their source not in nature, but in law[13].

Georg Wilhelm Hegel, the progressive philosopher, wrote: "the state (government) is the divine idea as it exists on earth." John Burgess, a prominent Progressive political scientist, wrote that the purpose of the state is the "perfection of humanity, the civilization of the world; the perfect development of the human reason and its attainment to universal command over individualism; the apotheosis of man" (man becoming God).

While the Founders believe in having restraints on the government to keep it from becoming too powerful—Woodrow Wilson disagrees. He criticized the Founders view that: "the ideal of government was for every man to be left alone and not interfered with, except when he interfered with somebody else; and that the best government was the government that did as little governing as possible." Wilson believed without government intervention men are at the mercy of the evil corporation. Wilson felt the poor would be destined to indefinite victimization by the wealthy. He believed limits on the federal government power must be abolished.

---

[12] Dewey, J., Boydston, J. A., & Ross, R. (2002). Reconstruction in philosophy and essays: 1920. Carbondale: Southern Illinois Univ. Pr.

[13] Watson, B. C. (2017). Progressive challenges to the American constitution: a new republic. Cambridge, United Kingdom: Cambridge University Press.

The flaw in Wilson's philosophy—while some corporations may take advantage of man, man can leave the corporation. When a powerful government takes advantage of man, he has no place to go. Progressive Theodore Woolsey wrote, "The sphere of the state may reach as far as the nature and needs of man and of men reach, including intellectual and aesthetic wants of the individual, and the religious and moral nature of its citizens." In progressivism, the government can never go too far. They can touch every aspect of your being, including your religious and moral beliefs.

Additional Policies of Progressivism:

The government must protect the poor and other victims of capitalism through redistribution of resources, anti-trust laws, government control over the details of commerce and production: i.e., dictating at what prices things must be sold, methods of manufacture, government participation in the banking system, and so on.

The government must become involved in the "spiritual" development of its citizens—not of course, through the promotion of religion, but through protecting the environment (conservation), education (understood as education to personal creativity), and spiritual uplift through subsidy and promotion of the arts and culture.

Turn power over to multinational organizations, such as Woodrow Wilson's plan for a League of Nations, under whose rules America would have delegated control over the deployment of its armed forces to that body.

Eliminate what they regarded as amateur politics. They believed modern science had superseded the perspective of the liberally educated statesman. Only people educated in the top universities, preferably in the social sciences, were thought to be capable of governing. Politics was regarded as too complex for common sense to cope with.

The government should take the responsibility of protecting the people against injuries and managing the entire economy while providing for the people's spiritual well-being. Only government agencies staffed by experts informed by the most advanced modern science could manage tasks previously handled within the private sphere. The government needed to be led by those who see where history is going and understand the ever-evolving idea of human dignity.

The Founders warned us against the welfare state, "cradle to the grave" mentality. They did all they could do to try to write the Constitution in a way to avoid moving towards a socialistic/communistic form of government. Jefferson wrote:

> *"If we can prevent the government from wasting the labors of the people, under the pretense of taking care of them, they must become happy." –Thomas Jefferson to T. Cooper, 1802.*

They also warned us against confiscatory (to take or seize someone's property with authority and give it to the public treasury) taxation and deficit spending. Jefferson wrote:

> *...we shall all consider ourselves unauthorized to saddle posterity (all future generations of people) with our debts, and morally bound to pay them ourselves: and consequently, within what may be deemed the period of a generation, or the life of the majority.*[14]

In other words, every generation is responsible for paying off their debt and not leave it for their children and grandchildren.

Today our national debt is over 21 trillion dollars. How did this get so bad? America has accumulated debt since the founding of our country. We can track the peaks and valleys during major events in our history. For instance, after the signing of our Constitution, the debt peek but was nearly paid off before the start of the Civil War. America incurred its second spike and was nearly paid off when World War I began. Again, we experienced another spike which subsided until World War II. Since WWII there has been little effort to lower our debt. There have been a few small declines but nothing worth commenting on. It's been a steady increase since.

The founders even warned against the ideas of socialism and communism. Samuel Adams said: "The Utopian schemes of leveling (re-distribution of wealth) and a community of goods

---

[14] Memorial Edition (Lipscomb and Bergh, editors)20 Vols., Washington, D.C., 1903-04.

(government owning the means of production and distribution), are as visionary and impractical as those which vest all property in the Crown." Adams goes on to say *"these ideas are arbitrate, despotic, and in our government, unconstitutional."*[15]

Progressive, Morris Fiorina, and others argue that when the government gets involved in providing extensive governmental programs for the public, politicians will win elections. The more government does, the easier it is to win votes and donations.

The Founders set up the Constitution to establish a limited government whose sole purpose is to protect the natural rights of the people of the United States. The natural rights are the key focal point against the progressive movement. The progressives know that if the people understand "natural rights" the movement cannot gain any traction. Natural rights come from God and therefore cannot be taken away by any person or government.

1880-1920 sparked the ground-breaking era of progressivism. Well-known figures such as Teddy Roosevelt and Woodrow Wilson address the Declaration of Independence and the Constitution in a manner to de-emphasize the foundational importance of these documents. In both of their speeches and writings, they attempt to de-legitimize the Founders and their beliefs.

For example, Woodrow Wilson, in an address honoring Thomas Jefferson stated: "if you want to understand the real Declaration of Independence, do not repeat the preface." To paraphrase, Wilson said: if you want to understand the Declaration of Independence just ignore the following parts: "...to assume among the powers of the earth, the separate and equal station to which the *Laws of Nature and of Nature's God* entitle them,..." and also ignore "...*all men are created equal,* that they are *endowed by their Creator* with certain unalienable Rights, that among these are Life, Liberty and the pursuit of Happiness.—That to secure these rights, *Governments are instituted among Men, deriving their just powers from the consent of the governed...*"

Three points to keep in mind. Wilson didn't believe:

---

[15] William V. Wells, The Life and Public Services of Samuel Adams, 3 volumes, Little, Brown and Company, Boston, 1865, 1:154

- That our power and rights come from the "Laws of Nature and of Nature's God.
- That all men are created equal and God gave us the rights of life, liberty and the pursuit of happiness—therefore no man or government can take these rights away from us.
- That the government's power comes from the people.

Wilson knew eliminating these three points from the American people's understanding was critical for the progressive movement to move forward. Progressives want you to believe that your rights are a blessing from the almighty government. Progressives need you to believe this to keep you from fighting for them when the government takes them away.

In summary, unlike our Founders, progressives don't believe man can self-govern themselves. Modern man is incapable of running their own lives. Should someone succeed, it's because the government assisted them the whole way. Therefore, they must re-distribute much of their wealth to 'help' others who couldn't succeed or were too lazy to succeed.

Progressivism needs people uneducated in our founding. They thrive on kayos, confusion, and division. They must control the narrative and squelch the opposition. If you were fortunate enough to go to an elite school to be indoctrinated in the proper ways of progressivism than you have a chance to be considered an elitist and may hold a seat in the prestigiously divine government.

Progressives are following the Cloward and Piven Strategy (by Richard Cloward and Frances Piven) and Saul Alinsky's book "Rules for Radicals." By researching these three individuals, you'll understand why America is struggling. You'll see it's by design and the plan is to take down our political and economic system.

The Administrative State

The administrative state is a tool of the progressive movement. It's designed to give more authority to the President while it takes authority from the people. Teddy Roosevelt, Woodrow Wilson and many presidents after them disliked the restraints the Constitution put on them. It limited their ability to "help" the American people as quickly and as efficiently as possible. Going through the congressional approval process was too burdensome for them. First, they decided to expand the use of the executive orders under the guise they were doing the people's work.

In Theodore Roosevelt's autobiography, he writes: "I declined to adopt the view that what was imperatively necessary for the Nation could not be done by the President unless he could find some specific authorization to do it. My belief was that it was not only his right but his duty to do anything that the needs of the Nation demanded unless such action was forbidden by the Constitution or by the laws. Under this interpretation of executive power, I did and caused to be done many things not previously done by the President and the heads of the departments. I did not usurp power, but I did greatly broaden the use of executive power. In other words, I acted for the public welfare; I acted for the common well-being of all our people, whenever and in whatever manner was necessary unless prevented by direct constitutional or legislative prohibition. I did not care a rap for the mere form and show of power; I cared immensely for the use that could be made of the substance...I believed in the people's rights, and therefore in National rights and States' rights just exactly to the degree in which they severally secured popular rights. I believed in invoking the National power with absolute freedom for every National need; and I believed that the Constitution should be treated as the greatest document ever devised by the wit of man to aid a people in exercising every power necessary for its own betterment, and not as a straitjacket cunningly fashioned to strangle growth..."[16]

Roosevelt made decisions 'he' felt were in the best interest of the people. He assumed the role of "king" and bypassed the people's representatives (Congress). Look at this from the modern-day perspective of former President Obama and now President Trump. Assuming both Presidents have America's best interest at heart. For eight years President Obama wrote executive orders which affected the people in many ways. We can say half the country was happy with his executive orders and half

---

[16] Theodore Roosevelt, "The Presidency: Making an Old Party Progressive," in The Rough Riders, An Autobiography (New York: The Macmillan Company, 1913), 614-15, 643

the country was not. But the 'king' made these decisions based on his perspective, and the country had to live with it.

Today President Trump is writing executive orders essentially overriding all President Obama's previous orders. Half of Americans are happy, and half are not. President Trump sees the country from a different perspective—and again, America must live with it.

What happens when the next President takes office? What perspective will he or she have? What will the American people have to deal with then? The Founders were very careful with the design and the words they chose in structuring the Constitution because they knew how power would corrupt leaders. Then they trusted the American people to elect men and women with high moral and virtuous character; who operates with strong Godly principles and have a powerful vision for America which they impart on people to follow. I would argue the American people dropped the ball regarding the politicians we have elected. Too many of our political men and women have little regard for moral principles and lack a strong, virtuous character. Look at what's in the news today: trading our vital uranium for personal profit; having a multi-million-dollar tax-funded slush fund for Congress to pay off victims of their own sexual miss-conduct; federal judges over-reaching their authority to essentially make laws or prevent another branch, the president, from exercising his Constitutional authority. This list could go on and on.

The second tool used is the administrative state. Agencies are established such as The Interstate Commerce Commission, the Internal Revenue Service, the Department of Education, the Food and the Drug Administration, Environmental Protection Agency, etc. These agencies internalize the governing bodies within its organization. Each body has un-elected bureaucrats, an executive, legislative and judicial working internally. They passed rules and regulations (laws) people and businesses must follow because they're enforced by the Executive Branch, the President, essentially bypassing Congress.

Since these departments answer directly to the President, he assumed all the power he wants. Affecting all areas of the American people's lives—clearly not what the Founders had intended. The President has the right to set these departments up.

However, any law they want to enact must pass through Congress first. This isn't how it currently works.

For example, former President Obama disliked the coal industry. Utilizing the EPA, he passed multiple rules and regulations which virtually shut down coal mines and would eventually put an end to coal. He desired to give an advantage to the solar and wind industry and used tax-payer funds to subsidize the industry—essentially taking more money from Americans and eliminates our freedom of choice.

President Obama might have accomplished his goals by using the proper channels. Present his case to Congress and ask them to pass a bill which would accomplish his agenda. After presenting his case to Congress, he could go and make the case to the American people. If his case were strong enough, the American people would put the pressure necessary on their Congressmen to pass the bill.

This wasn't an option for Obama because he knew the vast majority of people wouldn't approve. Instead, he played his "king" card and passed it by utilizing the administrative state. Now President Trump has reversed the rulings. Since President Obama chose to by-pass Congress, the only people hurt were the American people.

Essentially, both the 'executive orders' and the 'administrative state' have been used as powerful tools by the President to enact policies. These policies were important to the President's agenda but not the majority of Congress and the American people.

Chapter 4

God and Country

At the beginning of the book, I spoke about God's intervention into the founding of America. I told you America was built on the foundation of God—and that this is a Christian nation. In this chapter, you'll meet our Founders—what they stood for and why progressives dislike them. This is where the case for God begins.

For the progressive movement to succeed in changing America and enact their agenda—God must be eliminated. The principles of progressivism can't exist when the principles of God are present. Lies and distortions have been spread about our Founders to discredit their word and delegitimize the value of the Constitution they wrote.

The purpose of this chapter is to validate the Founders intentions. As you read their quotes and hear their stories, you'll know God played a huge part in forming this country. You'll know America was founded on Judeo-Christian principles and without God, we cannot stand. A republican form of government requires Godly principles to succeed.

There is a book called: America's God and Country Encyclopedia of Quotations by William J. Federer which I highly recommend. Many of the stories and quotes come directly from this book. It is seven hundred and ten pages of stories and quotes from our early beginnings right up to modern day as they pertain to God and America.

The quotes and stories chosen here are from our Founders only. Knowing who they were and what they stood for is important in understanding the original intent of the founding documents. They are listed in alphabetical order by the last name except for George Washington and Benjamin Franklin—which tell remarkable stories to set the stage.

Final note: The Holy Bible was found to have directly contributed to 34% of all quotes by the Founding Fathers. This was discovered after reviewing fifteen thousand items from the Founding Fathers (including newspaper articles, pamphlets, books, monographs, etc.). The other main sources the Founders quoted include Montesquieu, Blackstone, Locke, Pufendorf, etc., who themselves took 60% of their quotes directly from the Bible. Direct and indirect quotes combined reveal 94% of all the quotes of the Founding Fathers are derived from the Bible[17].

George Washington

During the French & Indian War, George Washington fought alongside British General Braddock. On July 9, 1755, the British were on the way to Fort Duquesne, when the French surprised them in an ambush attack.

The British, who were not accustomed to fighting unless in an open field, were being annihilated. Washington rode back and forth across the battle delivering General Braddock's orders. As the battle raged, every other officer on horseback, except Washington, was shot down. Even General Braddock was killed, at which point the troops fled in confusion. After the battle, on July 18, 1755, Washington wrote to his brother, John A. Washington[18]:

> *"But by the all-powerful dispensations of Providence, I have been protected beyond all human probability or expectation; for I had four bullets through my coat, and two horses shot under me, yet escaped unhurt, although death was leveling my companions on every side of me!"[19]*

Fifteen years later, Washington and Dr. Craik, a close friend, were traveling through those same woods near the Great Kanawha

---

[17] Holy Bible.1760-1805.Donald S. Lutz and Charles S. Hyneman, "The Relative Influence of European Writers on Late Eighteenth-Century American Political Thought," American Political Review 189 (1984):189-197

[18] Federer, W. J. (1994). America's God and Country. Coppell, Texas: Fame Publishing, Inc.

[19] July 18, 1755, in a letter to his brother. Jared Sparks, ed., The Writings of George Washington, 12 vols. (Boston; American Stationer's Company, 1837, NY; F. Andrew's 1834-1847), Vol. II, p.89

River and the Ohio River. They came across an old Indian chief, who, through an interpreter addressed Washington:

> *"I am a chief and ruler over my tribes. My influence extends to the waters of the Great Lakes and to the far Blue Mountains. I have traveled a long and weary path that I might see the young warrior of the great battle. It was on the day when the white man's blood mixed with the streams of our forests that I first beheld this chief (Washington). I called to my young men and said, mark yon tall and daring warrior? He is not of the red-coat tribe—he hath an Indian's wisdom, and his warriors fight as we do—himself alone exposed. Quick, let your aim be certain, and he dies. Our rifles were leveled, rifles which, but for you, knew not how to miss— 'twas all in vain, a power mightier far than we, shielded you. Seeing you were under the special guardianship of the Great Spirit, we immediately ceased to fire at you. I am old and soon shall be gathered to the great council fire of my fathers in the land of shades, but ere I go, there is something bids me speak in the voice of prophecy: Listen! The Great Spirit protects that man (pointing at Washington), and guides his destinies—he will become the chief of nations, and a people yet unborn will hail him as the founder of a mighty empire. I am come to pay homage to the man who is the particular favorite of Heaven, and who can never die in battle."[20]*

The Indian warrior, in that battle, said:

> *"Washington was never born to be killed by a bullet! I had seventeen fair fires at him with my rifle, and after all could not bring him to the ground."[21]*

What a remarkable story and this is only the beginning. George Washington didn't die in battle, and he did become the chief and Founder of a mighty empire called America.

---

[20] 1770. George Washington Parke Custis, Recollections and Private Memoirs of Washington, Benson J. Lossing, editor, (1860), p. 303

[21] 1770. David Barton, The Bulletproof George Washington (Aledo, TX; WallBuilder, Inc., Winter, 19930), p.49

The next story of George Washington is on August 27, 1776, British General Howe had trapped Washington and 8000 of his troops on Brooklyn Heights, Long Island. Being nightfall, Howe planned to advance his troops the next morning and crush them. Desperate, Washington gathered every vessel, from rowboats to fishing boats—spent all night ferrying his troops across the East River. By morning, there were still a large number of his army dangerously exposed to the British—but an unusual weather change occurred. The fog stayed thick and never lifted until Washington's entire army had evacuated the island! The British never had a better opportunity of winning the war[22].

Most of us learned in school about the unbearable times Washington's troops endured during the winter in Valley Forge. They didn't have blankets to cover themselves, and many didn't have shoes. We learned while they marched, the enemy could track them because of the blood in the snow from their bare feet. Washington records as many as twelve of his troops were dying each day due to the conditions. He wrote, regarding his men *"...and submitting without a murmur is a proof of patience and obedience which in my opinion can scarce be paralleled.[23]"*

When Washington and his troops were in Valley Forge, they camped on property owned by a Quaker named Isaac Potts. Quaker's didn't participate in wars, but Potts allowed Washington to set up camp on his land. Pott's is on record with the following story:

In 1777 while the American army lay at Valley Forge, a good old Quaker by the name of Potts had occasion to pass through thick woods near headquarters. As he traversed the dark brown forest, he heard, at a distance before him, a voice which as he advanced became more fervid and interested. Approaching with slowness and circumspection, whom should he behold in a dark bower, apparently formed for the purpose, but the Commander-in-Chief of the armies of the

---

[22] Aug 27, 1776. John Fiske, The American Revolution, 2 vols. (Boston and New York Houghton, Mifflin & Co., 1898), p. 212

[23] In a letter written from Valley Forge to John Banister, dated April 21, 1778. William Barclay Allen, ed., George Washington—A Collection (Indianapolis; Liberty Classics, Liberty Fund, Inc., 7440 N. Shadeland, Indianapolis, In. 1988

United Colonies on his knees in the act of devotion to the Ruler of the Universe!

At the moment when Friend Potts, concealed by the trees came up, Washington was interceding for his beloved country. With tones of gratitude that labored for adequate expression he adored that exuberant goodness which, from the depth of obscurity, had exalted him to the head of a great nation, and that nation fighting at fearful odds for all the world holds dear...

Soon as the General had finished his devotions and had retired, Friend Potts returned to his house, and threw himself into a chair by the side of his wife. "Heigh! Isaac!" said she with tenderness, "thee seems agitated; what's the matter?"

"Indeed, my dear" quoth he, "if I appear agitated 'tis no more than what I am. I have seen this day what I shall never forget. Till now I have thought that a Christian and a soldier were characters incompatible; but if George Washington be not a man of God, I am mistaken, and still more shall I be disappointed if God does not through him perform some great thing for this country."[24]

On May 12, 1779, General George Washington was visited at his Middle Brook military encampment by the Chiefs of the Delaware Indian tribe. They had brought three youths to be trained in American schools. Washington assured them, commenting:[25]

"Congress will look upon them as their own Children...You do well to wish to learn our arts and ways of life, and above all, the religion of Jesus Christ. These will make you a greater and happier people than you are. Congress will do everything they can to assist you in this wise intention."[26]

---

[24] Winter of 1777, Washington's Prayer observed by Isaac Potts, recounted by Ruth Anna Potts. William Herbert Burk, D.D., The Washington Window in the Washington Memorial Chapel of Valley Forge, p. 25

[25] Federer, W. J. (1994). America's God and Country. Coppell, Texas: Fame Publishing, Inc. p. 643-644

[26] May 12, 1779, from his "Address to Delaware Chiefs Indian Chiefs," John Clement Fitzpatrick, ed., The Writings of George Washington from the Original Manuscript Sources: 1749-1799, 39 vols (Washington D.C. Bureau of National Literature and Art, 1907), 1:65

Look at the last page of the Constitution you will notice George Washington signed the Constitution as President of Continental Convention and played a leading role in the creation of the Constitution. Does Washington's comments above sound like he or Congress believe religion should not play a role in our government? The Founders believed a republican government could never survive without the Christian religion playing a key role in government. Modern-day progressives will have you believe otherwise.

Do you know the story behind Benedict Arnold as a traitor? On Monday, September 25, 1780, Benedict Arnold, Commander of West Point, plotted to betray the Continental Army into the hands of the British. George Washington responded to this miraculous deliverance by issuing the following circular to his troops: He writes:[27]

> *"Treason of the blackest dye was yesterday discovered! General Arnold who commanded at WestPoint, lost to every sentiment of honor, of public and private obligation, was about to deliver up that important Post into the hands of the enemy. Such an event must have given the American Cause a deadly wound if not fatal stab. Happily, the treason had been timely discovered to prevent the fatal misfortune. The providential train of circumstances which led to it affords the most convincing proof that the Liberties of America are the object of divine Protection."[28]*

Washington wrote about many miracles that occurred during the war with Britain. He explains three or four separate times they were being pursued by the British—and the American troops would just get across a river and something miraculous would occur where the water would rise to heights that made it unbearable for the British troops to get across in their pursuit. The British Commander-in-Chief Henry Clinton wrote, explaining the incident:[29]

---

[27] Federer, W. J. (1994). America's God and Country. Coppell, Texas: Fame Publishing, Inc. p. 645

[28] September 26, 1780, Tuesday, in his General Orders from his headquarters in Orangetown, John Clement Fitzpatrick, ed., The Writings of George Washington, from the Original Manuscript Sources 1749-1799, 39 vols. (Washington, D.C.: U.S. Government Printing Office, 1931-1944), Vol. XX, pp.94-95

[29] Federer, W. J. (1994). America's God and Country. Coppell, Texas: Fame Publishing, Inc. p.645-646

"Here the royal army was again stopped by a sudden rise of the waters, which had only just fallen (almost miraculously) to let the enemy over, who could not else have eluded Lord Cornwallis' grasp, so close was he upon their rear".[30]

As President of the United States, George Washington speaks of God and the need for His Divine Presence throughout his speeches, writings, and his personal journals. His Inaugural Address, his National Day of Thanksgiving Proclamation, his annual addresses to the nation, writings to different churches are all full of his acknowledgment of the intervention of God and the recognition of our nation's need for Him and His Divine presence.

These are a small sampling of the writings of George Washington. His faith and impeccable belief in God are above reproach. Many books have been written about Washington and his Godly character. He wrote a book or journal of his own personal prayers. There's one prayer for the morning and one for the evening for each day of the week. Here is his Sunday evening prayer:

"O most Glorious God, in Jesus Christ my merciful and loving Father, I acknowledge and confess my guilt, in the weak and imperfect performance of the duties of this day. I have called on Thee for pardon and forgiveness of sins...Let me live according to those holy rules which Thou hast this day prescribed in Thy holy word; make me to know what is acceptable in Thy sight, and therein to delight, open the eyes of my understanding, and help me thoroughly increase my faith, and direct me to the true object, Jesus Christ the Way, the Truth and the Life, bless, O Lord, all the people of this land, from the highest to the lowest, particularly those whom Thou hast appointed to rule us in church & state. Continue Thy goodness to me this night. These weak petitions, I

---

[30] February 13, 1781, in a report from British Commander-in-Chief Henry Clinton. William Hosmer, Remember our Bicentennial—1781 (Foundation for Christian Self-Government Newsletter—June 1981), p. 5.

humbly implore Thee to hear, accept and answer for the sake of Thy Dear Son, Jesus Christ our Lord, Amen[31].

Benjamin Franklin

Ben Franklin was an inventor, a scientist, a politician, a writer, and a printer. He is famous for writing annual publications called Poor Richard's Almanac. His writings included:

*"God heals, and the doctor takes the fees[32]
"God helps them that help themselves"[33]
"Work as if you were to live 100 years; pray as if you were to die tomorrow"[34]*

His autobiography states he prayed this prayer every day:

"O powerful goodness! Bountiful Father! Merciful Guide! Increase in me that wisdom which discovers my truest interest. Strengthen my resolution to perform what that wisdom dictates. Accept my kind offices to thy other children as the only return in my power for thy continual favors to me."[35]

Here are a few of his lessons from his Maxims and Morals, Benjamin Franklin wrote:

- *Search others for their virtues, thy self for thy vices.*
- *Keep your eyes open before marriage, half shut afterwards.*
- *My father convinced me that nothing was useful which was not honest.*
- *Freedom is not a gift bestowed upon us by other men, but a right that belongs to us by the laws of God and nature.*
- *Remember Job (from the Old Testament) suffered and was afterwards prosperous.*

---

[31]Journal of Senate and House, 3rd Congress, 2nd Session. November 19, 1794, in his sixth annual message to Congress. American State Papers, Miscellaneous, (complete text), Vol. I, p. 83-85

[32] Poor Richard's Almanac. Carroll E. Simcox, comp.,4400 Quotations for Christian Communicators (Grand Rapids, Mi: Baker Book House, 1991), p. 185

[33] 1733, in Poor Richards's Almanac. Raymond A. St. John, American Literature for Christian Schools (Greenville, SC: Bob Jones University Press, Inc., 1979), p. 126

[34] May 1757, in Poor Richard's Almanac. Carroll E. Simcox, comp., 4400 Quotations for Christian Communicators (Grand Rapids, MI: Baker Book House, 1991), p. 297

[35]The Autobiography of Benjamin Franklin. Norman Cousins, In God We Trust—The Religious Beliefs and Ideas of the American Founding Fathers (NY: Harper & Brothers, Publishers, 1955), p.30

- ■ *I never doubted the existence of the Deity that he made the world and governed it by His Providence.*
- ■ *The pleasures of this world are rather from God's goodness than our own merit[36].*

Ben Franklin was appointed part of a committee, in July 1776 to draft a seal for the newly declared United States that would characterize the spirit of the nation. He proposed:

> *Moses lifting his staff, and dividing the red sea, and pharaoh in his chariot overwhelmed with the waters. This moto: "Rebellion to tyrants is obedience to God."[37]*

In a letter to Ezra Stiles, President of Yale University, Franklin writes:

> *"Here is my creed: I believe in one God, the Creator of the universe. That he governs it by his providence. That he ought to be worshipped. That the most acceptable service we render to him is in doing good to his other children. That the soul of man is immortal, and will be treated with justice in another life respecting its conduct in this..."[38]*

In a letter to the French ministry on March 1778 Ben Franklin wrote:

> *"Whoever shall introduce into public affairs the principles of primitive Christianity will change the face of the world."[39]*

In a pamphlet Ben Franklin wrote entitled "Information to Those Who Would Remove to America" written for Europeans who were

---

[36] William S. Pfaff, ed., Maxims and Morals of Benjamin Franklin (New Orleans: Searcy and Pfaff, Ltd., 1927).

[37] August 14, 1776. Charles Francis Adams (son of John Quincy Adams and grandson of John Adams), ed., Letters of John Adams, Addressed to His Wife, (Boston: Charles C. Little and James Brown, 1841), Vol. I p. 152

[38] Smyth, Writings of Benjamin Franklin, 10:84.

[39] David Barton, The Myth of Separation (Aledo, TX: WallBuilder Press, 1991), p. 151

considering the move to America or were planning on sending their children he states:[40]

> *"Hence bad examples to youth are more rare in America, which must be a comfortable consideration to parents. To this may be truly added, that serious religion, under its various denominations, is not only tolerated, but respected and practiced.*
>
> *Atheism is unknown there' Infidelity rare and secret; so that persons may live to a great age in that country without having their piety shocked by meeting with either an Atheist or an Infidel.*
>
> *And the Divine Being seems to have manifested his approbation of the mutual forbearance and kindness with which the different sects treat each other; by the remarkable prosperity with which He has been pleased to favor the whole country."[41]*

During the Constitutional Convention, the delegates were in very hostile arguments over how each state would be represented. This was so much the case that many of the delegates left the convention. Ben Franklin stood up to speak:

Mr. President:

> *The small progress we have made after four or five weeks close attendance and continual reasoning with each other- our different sentiments on almost every question, several of the last producing as many noes as ayes, is methinks a melancholy proof of the imperfection of the Human Understanding.*
>
> *We indeed seem to feel our own want of political wisdom, since we have been running about in search of it. We have gone back to ancient history for models of government, and examined the different forms of republic which, having been formed with the seeds of their own dissolution, now no longer exist. And we have viewed Modern States all round*

---

[40] Federer, W. J. (1994). America's God and Country. Coppell, Texas: Fame Publishing, Inc. p. 247
[41] Benjamin Franklin, Information on Those Who Would Remove to America (London: M. Gurney, 1954). Pp.22,23

Europe, but find none of their Constitutions suitable to our circumstances.

In this situation of this Assembly, groping as it were in the dark to find political truth, and scarce able to distinguish it when presented to us, how has it happened, Sir, that we have not hitherto once thought of humbly applying to the Father of lights to illuminate our understanding?

In the beginning of the contest with Great Britain, when we were sensible of danger, we had daily prayer in this room for Divine protection. Our prayers, Sir, were heard, and they were graciously answered. All of us who were engaged in the struggle must have observed frequent instances of a superintending Providence in our favor.

To that kind Providence we owe this happy opportunity of consulting in peace on the means of establishing our future national felicity. And have we now forgotten that powerful Friend? Or do we imagine we no longer need His assistance?

I have lived, Sir, a long time, and the longer I live, the more convincing proofs I see of this truth—that God Governs in the affairs of men. And if a sparrow cannot fall to the ground without His notice, is it probable that an empire can rise without His aid?

We have been assured, Sir, in the Sacred Writings, that "except the Lord build the House, they labor in vain that build it." I firmly believe this; and I also believe that without his concurring aid we shall succeed in this political building no better than the builders of Babel. We shall be divided by our partial local interests; our projects will be confounded, and we ourselves shall become a reproach and bye word down to future ages.

And what is worse, mankind may hereafter from this unfortunate instance, despair of establishing Governments by Human wisdom and leave it to chance, war and conquest. I therefore beg leave to move-that henceforth prayers imploring the assistance of Heaven, and its blessing on our deliberations, be held in this Assembly every morning before we proceed to business, and that one or more of the clergy of this city be requested to officiate in that service.[42]

Because of the above speech, the Convention continued and formed what we now call the Constitution of the United States of America and prayer still opens every house of Congress to this day.

In the Old Testament Book of Joshua, after Moses had brought the Israelites to the Promised Land, Joshua and the Israelites were in the midst of conquering the different Kingdoms that occupied the land God had given them. They conquered the town of Gibeon which was one of the royal cities. Five Kings of that nation got together to take back Gibeon from Joshua. During the fight, Joshua asked God to cause the sun and the moon to remain out so they could finish the job of destroying the enemy of the Israelites. "The sun stopped in the middle of the sky and delayed going down about a full day." I shared this Biblical story, so the next story of Franklin makes sense to anyone not familiar with who Joshua was.

Ben Franklin was ambassador to the United States; he attended a dinner of foreign dignitaries in Versailles, France. The minister of Great Britain proposed a toast to King George III, likening him to the sun. The French minister, in like kind, proposed a toast to King Louis XVI, comparing him with the moon. Ben Franklin stood up and toasted:[43] *"George Washington, Commander of the American armies, who like Joshua of old, commanded the sun and the moon to stand still, and they obeyed him."*[44]

Most if not all the Founders were Godly men and believed in the God of the Universe. The progressive movement has forced these and other writings into secrecy to promote their agenda. It's time the word got back out. We'll close Ben Franklin's quotes with the epitaph he wrote for himself:

---

[42] Benjamin Franklin. June 28, 1787. James Madison, Notes of Debates in the Federal Convention of 1787 (NY: W.W. Morton & Co., Original 1787 reprinted 1987), Vol. I, p. 504, 451-21.

[43] Federer, W. J. (1994). America's God and Country. Coppell, Texas: Fame Publishing, Inc. p.250

[44] In a toast at a dinner of foreign ambassadors in Versailles, France. John Bartlett, Bartlett's Familiar Quotations (Boston: Little, Brown and Company, 1855, 1980), p. 348

THE BODY
Of
BENJAMIN FRANKLIN
Printer
Like the cover of an old book,
Its contents torn out,
And stripped of its lettering and gilding
Lays here, food for worms;
Yet the work itself shall not be lost,
For it will (as he believed) appear once more,
In a new,
And more beautiful edition,
Corrected and amended
By The AUTHOR[45]

John Adams

John Adams wrote in his diary on February 22, 1756, twenty years before he signed the Declaration of Independence:

Suppose a nation in some distant region should take the Bible for their only law book, and every member should regulate his conduct by the precepts there exhibited! Every member would be obliged in conscience, to temperance, frugality, and industry; to justice, kindness, and charity towards his fellow men; and to piety, love, and reverence toward Almighty God.... What a Eutopia, what a Paradise would this region be.[46]

On July 1, 1776, John Adams spoke to the Continental Congress:

Before God, I believe the hour has come. My judgment approves this measure, and my whole heart is in it. All that I have, and all that I am, and all that I hope in this life, I am now ready here to stake upon it. And I leave off as I began, that live or die, survive or perish, I am for the Declaration. It is my living sentiment, and by the blessing of God it shall be

---

[45] Benjamin Franklin. 1728, in his "Articles of Belief and Acts of Religion. "Jared Sparks, ed., The Writings of Benjamin Franklin (Boston: Tappan, Whittemore and Mason, 1840), Vol. II, PP. 1-3.
[46] John Adams. February 22, 1756, in a diary entry. L.H. Butterfield, ed., Diary and Autobiography of John Adams (Cambridge, MA: Belknap Press of Harvard Press, 1961), Vol. III, p.9

my dying sentiment. Independence now and Independence for ever.[47]

On July 3, 1776, John Adams wrote to his wife Abigail (see if this describes our July 4th celebration):

"The second day of July 1776, will be the most memorable epoch in the history of America. I am apt to believe that it will be celebrated by succeeding generations as the great anniversary Festival. It ought to be commemorated, as the Day of Deliverance, by solemn acts of devotion to God Almighty. It ought to be solemnized with pomp and parade, with shows, games, sports, guns, bell, bonfires and illuminations, from one end of this continent to the other, from this time forward forever.

You will think me transported with enthusiasm, but I am not. I am well aware of the toil and blood and treasure that it will cost to maintain this Declaration, and support and defend these States. Yet through all the gloom I can see the rays of ravishing light and glory. I can see that the end is worth more than all the means; that posterity will triumph in that day's transaction, even though we (may regret) it, which I trust in God we shall not".[48]

On July 26, 1796, John Adams wrote in his diary:

The Christian religion is, above all the religions that ever prevailed or existed in ancient or modern times, the religion of Wisdom, Virtue, Equity, and Humanity.[49]

In his Inaugural Address, President Adams said:

...and may that Being who is supreme over all, the Patron of Order, the Fountain of Justice, and the Protector in all ages

---

[47] John Adams. July 1, 1776, in speaking to the delegates at the Continental Congress. William H. McGuffey, McGuffey's Eclectic Fifth Reader (NY: American Book Company, 1907; revised 1920), p.199

[48] John Adams. July 3, 1776, in a letter t his wife Abigail, in relation to the state of the Cause of Independence. Charles Francis Adams (son of John Quincy Adams and grandson of John Adams), ed., Letters of John Adams-Addressed to His Wife (Boston: Charles C. Little and James Brown, 1841), Vol I, p. 128

[49] John Adams. July 26, 1796, Norman Cousins, In God We Trust—The Religious Beliefs and Ideas of the American Founding Fathers (NY: Harper & Brothers, 1958), p. 99

of the world virtuous liberty, continue His blessings upon this nation.[50]

A prayer that John Adams composed while writing his wife is engraved on the mantel in the state dining room of the White House to this day:

> *I pray Heaven to bestow THE BEST OF BLESSINGS ON THIS HOUSE and All that shall hereafter inhabit it, May none but Honest and Wise Men ever rule under this roof.[51]*

In a letter written to Mr. Warren, John Adams explains the importance of religion, moral values, and virtue in the republican form of government. John writes:

> *This form of Government...is productive of everything which is great and excellent among men. But its Principles are as easily destroyed; as human nature is corrupted...A Government is only to be supported by pure Religion or Austere Morals. Private and public Virtue is the only Foundation of Republics.[52]*

Another letter to Thomas Jefferson he writes:

> *I have examined all religions, as well as my narrow sphere, my straightened means, and my busy life, would allow; and the result is that the Bible is the best Book in the world. It contains more philosophy than all the libraries I have seen.[53]*

---

[50] John Adams. March 4, 1797, in his Inaugural Address. Proclaim Liberty (Dallas, TX: Word of Faith), p. 1.

[51] John Adams. November 1800, in a letter to his wife, Abigail, in which he composed a prayer. John Adams, John Adam's Prayer (Washington, D.C.: White House Collection, engraved upon the mantel, state dining room). John Bartlett, Bartlett's Familiar Quotations (Boston: Little, Brown and Company, 1855, 1980), p. 382

[52] John Adams. In a letter to Mr. Warren. Warren-Adams Letters (Boston, MA: Massachusetts Historical Society, 1917), Vol. I p. 222.

[53] John Adams. December 25, 1813, in a letter to Thomas Jefferson. Norman Cousins, In God We Trust— The Religious Beliefs and Ideas of the American Founding Fathers (NY: Harper & Brothers, 1958), p. 256

Still another letter to Thomas Jefferson he writes: *The Ten Commandments and the Sermon on the Mount contain my religion...[54]*

Clearly, John Adams believed the Christian religion was of utmost importance in governing of this nation. Believing the Founders wanted to keep the Christian religion out of schools and the public square is the work of the religion of atheism and progressivism.

Interesting fact: On July 4, 1826, Independence Day, exactly fifty years after John Adams and Thomas Jefferson signed the Declaration of Independence, they both died.

Samuel Adams

Samuel Adams, in his publication, called: The Rights of the Colonists, in 1772 writes:

> *The right to freedom being the gift of the Almighty...The rights of the colonists as Christians...may be best understood by reading and carefully studying the institution of The Great Law Giver and Head of the Christian Church, which are to be found clearly written and promulgated in the New Testament.[55]*

After the signing of the Declaration of Independence in 1776, Sam Adams declared:

> *We have this day restored the Sovereign to Whom all men ought to be obedient. He reigns in heaven and from the rising to the setting of the sun, let His kingdom come.[56]*

In a letter Sam Adams wrote to his cousin John Adams who at the time was the Vice President of the United States under President George Washington:

> *Let divines and philosophers, statesmen and patriots, unite their endeavors to renovate the age, by impressing the minds*

---

[54] John Adams. November 4, 1816, in a letter to Thomas Jefferson (1812-1826) (Indianapolis: The Bobbs-Merrill Publishers, 1925), p. 112

[55] Samuel Adams. November 20, 1772, in his pamphlet entitled, The Rights of the Colonists, in section: "The Rights of the Colonist as Christians." The Rights of the Colonists (Boston: Old South Leaflets), Vol. VII 1772.

[56] Samuel Adams. 1776, statement made while the Declaration of Independence was being signed. Charles E. Kistler, This Nation Under God (Boston: Richard G. Badger, The Gorham Press, 1924), p. 71

of men with the importance of educating their little boys and girls, of inculcating in the minds of youth the fear and love of the Deity and universal philanthropy, and, in subordination to these great principles, the love of their country; of instructing them in the art of self-government without which they never can act a wise part in the government of societies, great or small; in short, of leading them in the study and practice of the exalted virtues of the Christian system.[57]

On March 20, 1797, while Governor of Massachusetts, Samuel Adams declared:

I conceive we cannot better express ourselves than by humbly supplicating the Supreme Ruler of the world... that the confusions that are and have been among the nations may be overruled by the promoting and speedily bringing in the holy and happy period when the kingdoms of our Lord and Saviour Jesus Christ may be everywhere established, and the people willingly bow to the scepter of Him who is the Prince of Peace.[58]

Fisher Ames

Fisher Ames was a Congressman from Massachusetts who suggested the wording for the First Amendment in the Constitution. He states in an article published in Palladium magazine on September 20, 1789:

We have a dangerous trend beginning to take place in our education. We're starting to put more and more textbooks into our schools...We've become accustomed of late to putting little books into the hands of children containing fables and moral lessons... We are spending less time in the classroom on the Bible, which should be the principle text in

---

[57] Samuel Adams. October 4, 1790, in a letter to his cousin, Vice-President John Adams. Four Letters: Being as Interesting Correspondence Between...John Adams...and Samuel Adams (Boston: Adams & Rhoades, 1802)
[58] Samuel Adams. March 20, 1797, as Governor of Massachusetts, in a Proclamation of a Day of Fast. Cushing, ed., The Writings of Samuel Adams, II:355-56

our schools... The Bible states these great moral lessons better than any other manmade book.[59]

Richard Bassett and Gunning Bedford

Richard Bassett and Gunning Bedford both signed the Constitution of the United States and participated in the writing of the Constitution of the State of Delaware, which states:

> *Article XXII Every person who shall be chosen a member of either house, or appointed to any office or place of trust...shall...make and subscribe the following declaration, to wit: "I,_______, do profess faith in God the Father, and in Jesus Christ His only Son, and in the Holy Ghost, one God, blessed for evermore; and I do acknowledge the holy scriptures of the Old and New Testament to be given by divine inspiration.*[60]

Samuel Chase

Samuel Chase signed the Declaration of Independence and was appointed as a Supreme Court Justice by George Washington. In one of his court's opinion he writes:

> *Religion is of general and public concern, and on its support depend, in great measure, the peace and good order of government, the safety and happiness of the people. By our form of government, the Christian religion is the established religion; and all sects and denominations of Christians are placed upon the same equal footing and are equally entitled to protection in their religious liberty.*[61]

John Dickinson

John Dickinson signed the Constitution of the United States and was called the Penman of the Revolution. Several months

---

[59] Fisher Ames. September 20, 1789, in an article published in Palladium magazine. D. James Kennedy, "The Great Deception" (Fort Lauderdale, Florida: Coral Ridge Ministries, 1989; 1993), p. 3

[60] Richard Bassett. 1776, Constitution of the State of Delaware, Article 22. The Constitution of the Several Independent States of America—Published by Order of Congress (Boston: Norman & Bowen, 1785), pp. 99-100.

[61] Samuel Chase. Runkel v. Winemiller, 4 Harris & McHenry 276, 288 (Sup. Ct. Md. 1799). Runkel v. Winemiller, 4 Harris & McHenry (MD) 429 1 AD 411, 417

before the Declaration of Independence was signed, he suggested requirements for the members of the Convention to subscribe to the following stipulations:

> *I do profess faith in God the Father, and in Jesus Christ his Eternal Son the true God, and in the Holy Spirit, one God blessed for evermore; and I do acknowledge the Holy Scriptures of the Old and New Testaments to be given by Divine inspiration.*[62]

Alexander Hamilton

Alexander Hamilton signed the Constitution of the United States and wrote most of the Federalist papers. Shortly after the Constitutional Convention of 1787, he stated the following:

> *For my own part, I sincerely esteem it a system which without the finger of God, never could have been suggested and agreed upon by such a diversity of interests.*[63]

In writing to a friend named James Bayard in April of 1802, Hamilton wrote:

> *In my opinion, the present Constitution is the standard to which we are to cling. Under its banner bona fide must we combat our political foes, rejecting all changes but through the channel itself provided for amendments. By these general views of the subject have my reflections been guided. I now offer you the outline of the plan they have suggested. Let an association be formed to be denominated "The Christian Constitutional Society," its object to be first: The support of the Christian religion, second: The support of the United States.*[64]

Continuing, Hamilton wrote:

---

[62] John Dickinson. 1768, in The Liberty Song. John Bartlett, Bartlett's Familiar Quotations (Boston: Little, Brown and Co, 1863, 1980), p. 378

[63] Alexander Hamilton 1787. Christine F. Hart, One Nation Under God (NJ: American Tract Society, reprinted by Gospel Tract Society, Inc), p. 2

[64] Alexander Hamilton. April 16-21, 1802, in writing to James Bayard. Claude G. Bowers, Jefferson and Hamilton: The Struggle for Democracy in America (Boston: Houghton Mifflin Co., 1925, 1937), p. 40

I have carefully examined the evidences of the Christian religion, and if I was sitting as a juror upon its authenticity I would unhesitatingly give my verdict in its favor. I can prove its truth as clearly as any proposition ever submitted to the mind of man.[65]

John Hancock

John Hancock was the first person to sign the Declaration of Independence. On April 15, 1775, he declared A Day of Public Humiliation, Fasting and Prayer stating:

In circumstances dark as these, it becomes us, as Men and Christians, to reflect that, whilst every prudent Measure should be taken to ward off the impending Judgements...All confidence must be withheld from the Means we use; and reposed only on that GOD who rules in the Armies of Heaven, and without whose Blessing the best human Counsels are but Foolishness—and all created Power Vanity;
It is the Happiness of his Church that, when the Powers of Earth and Hell combine against it...that the Throne of Grace is of the easiest access—and its Appeal thither is graciously invited by the Father of Mercies, who has assured it, that when his Children ask Bread he will not give them a Stone...
Resolved, that it be, and hereby is recommended to the good People of this Colony of all Denominations, that Thursday the Eleventh Day of May next be set apart as a Day of Public Humiliation, Fasting and Prayer...to confess the sins...to implore the Forgiveness of all our Transgressions... and a blessing on the Husbandry, Manufactures, and other lawful Employments of this People; and especially that the union of the American Colonies in Defense of their Rights (for hitherto we desire to thank Almighty GOD) may be preserved and confirmed...And that America may soon behold a gracious Interposition of Heaven.[66]

---

[65] Alexander Hamilton. Sarah K. Bolton, Famous American Statesmen, p. 126
[66] John Hancock. April 15, 1775, Massachusetts Provincial Congress declaring a Day of Public Humiliation, Fasting and Prayer. Proclamation of John Hancock from Concord (from an original in the Evans collection, #14220, by the American Antiquarian Society)

Patrick Henry

Patrick Henry did not sign either the Declaration of Independence or the Constitution but was a major player in the Revolutionary War. With mounting tension between the Colonies and the British Crown, on March 23, 1775, Patrick Henry gave his fiery patriotic speech which he ended as follows:

> *...Is life so dear, or peace so sweet, as to be purchased at the price of chains and slavery? Forbid it, Almighty God! I know not what course others may take; but as for me, give me liberty or give me death.*[67]

Patrick Henry boldly declared:

> *It cannot be emphasized too strongly or too often that this great nation was founded, not by religionist, but by Christians; not on religions, but on the Gospel of Jesus Christ. For this very reason peoples of other faiths have been afforded asylum, prosperity and freedom of worship here.*[68]

In Patrick Henry's Last Will and Testament, he writes:

> *This is all the inheritance I give to my dear family. The religion of Christ will give them one which will make them rich indeed.*[69]

John Jay

John Jay did not sign either the Declaration of Independence or the Constitution but was very instrumental in getting the Constitution ratified by assisting in the writings of the Federalist papers. He was appointed by President Washington to

---

[67] Patrick Henry. March 23, 1775, in The Second Virginia Convention given at St. John's Church in Richmond Virginia. Catherine Millard, The Rewriting of America's History (Camp Hill, PA: Horizon House Publishers, 1991), pp. 131-135.

[68] Patrick Henry. Steve C. Dawson, God's Providence in America's History (Rancho Cordova, CA: Steve C. Dawson, 1988) Vol. I p. 5

[69] Patrick Henry. November 20, 1798, in a Certified Copy of Last Will and Testament of Patrick Henry. William Wirt Henry, Patrick Henry: Life, Correspondence and Speeches (NY: Charles Scribner's Sons, 1891), Vol. II, p. 631

be the first Chief Justice of the Supreme Court. On October 12, 1816, John Jay stated:

> *Providence has given to our people the choice of their rulers, and it is the duty, as well as the privilege and interest of our Christian nation to select and prefer Christians for their rulers.*[70]

In John Jay's Last Will and Testament, he writes:

> *Unto Him who is the author and giver of all good, I render sincere and humble thanks for His merciful and unmerited blessings, and especially for our redemption and salvation by his beloved Son.*[71]

Thomas Jefferson

Shortly after the signing of the Declaration of Independence, Jefferson, like Ben Franklin was appointed to the committee to draft a seal for the United States. His suggestion was: The children of Israel in the wilderness, led by a cloud by day, and a pillar of fire by night.[72]

In his notes on the State of Virginia 1781, Thomas Jefferson writes:

> *God who gave us life gave us liberty. And can the liberties of a nation be thought secure when we have removed their only firm basis, a conviction in the minds of the people that these liberties are of the Gift of God? That they are not to be violated but with His wrath? Indeed, I tremble for my country when I reflect that God is just; that His justice cannot sleep forever.*[73]

On April 30, 1802, Thomas Jefferson signed the Northwest Ordinance. Article III of that ordinance states:

---

[70] John Jay. October 12, 1816, in a statement. The Correspondence and Public Papers of John Jay, Henry P. Johnston, ed., (NY: Burt Franklin, 1970), Vol. IV, p. 393.

[71] John Jay. In his Last Will and Testament. William Jay, The Life of John Jay with Selections from His Correspondence, 3 vols. (New York: Harper, 1833), Vol. I pp. 519-520.

[72] Thomas Jefferson. July 3, 1776, in a proposition for a national seal. Journals of the Continental Congress, 1776, Vol. V p. 530

[73] Thomas Jefferson. 1781, in his Notes on the State of Virginia, Query XVII, 1781, 1782, p. 237

Religion, morality, and knowledge being necessary to good government and the happiness of mankind, schools and the means of education shall be forever encouraged.[74]

President Thomas Jefferson extended, three times, a 1787 act of Congress in which special lands were designated: For the sole use of Christian Indians and the Moravian Brethren missionaries for civilizing the Indians and promoting Christianity.[75]
Jefferson declared that religion is:

Deemed in other countries incompatible with good government and yet proved by our experience to be its best support.[76]

John Langdon

John Langdon signed the Constitution of the United States. He was Governor of New Hampshire and a colonel in the militia. As Governor he made two official Proclamations: One for a day of General Thanksgiving; and one for a Day of Public Fasting and Prayer. He was also one of the Founders and first President of the New Hampshire Bible Society. In 1817 John Langdon was visited by President James Monroe. The local newspaper wrote the following article:[77]

While at Portsmouth, the President spent that part of the Sabbath which was not devoted to public divine service, with that eminent patriot and Christian, John Langdon. His tarry at the mansion of the Governor was probably longer than the time devoted to any individual in New England. It is thus that the President has evinced his partiality to our most distinguished and illustrious citizen.[78]

---

[74] Thomas Jefferson. April 30, 1802, c.40, 2 Stat. 173 at 174. David Barton, The Myth of Separation (Aledo, TX: WallBuilder Press, 1991), p. 38

[75] Thomas Jefferson. December 3, 1803, treaty with the Kaskaskia Indians, 1806 with the Wyandotte Indians, and 1807 Cherokee Indians. Daniel L. Driesbach, Real Threat and Mere Shadow: Religious Liberty and the First Amendment (Westchester, IL: Crossway Books, 1987), p. 127

[76] Thomas Jefferson. Stephen K McDowell and Mark A. Beliles, America's Providential History (Charlottesville, VA: Providence Press, 1988), p. 148

[77] Federer, W. J. (1994). America's God and Country. Coppell, Texas: Fame Publishing, Inc. pp. 357-60

[78] Thomas Babington, Lord Macaulay. 1837, in writing On Lord Bacon. John Bartlett, Bartlett's Familiar Quotations (Boston: Little, Brown and Company, 1855, 1980), p. 488

William Livingston

William Livingston signed the Constitution of the United States and was the first Governor of New Jersey. While living in New York, he published many articles in The Independent Reflector, such as No. 46:

> *I believe the Scriptures of the Old and New Testaments, without any foreign comments or human explanations...I believe that he who feareth God and worketh righteousness will be accepted of Him...I believe that the virulence of some...proceeds not from their affection to Christianity, which is founded on too firm a basis to be shaken by the freest inquiry, and the Divine authority of which I sincerely believe without receiving a farthing for saying so.*[79]

In a letter, William Livingston wrote:

> *If the history (New Testament) be not true, then all the whole laws of nature were changed; all the motives and incentives to human actions that ever had obtained in this world have been entirely inverted; the wickedest men in the world have taken the greatest pains and endured the greatest hardship and misery to invent, practice, and propagate the most holy religion that ever was.*[80]

James Madison

James Madison signed the Constitution of the United States and was considered the "Chief Architect" of the Constitution. He also wrote 29 of the Federalist Papers. On June 20, 1785, he wrote: *Religion is the basis and foundation of government.*[81]

James Madison's writing on the future of America:

---

[79] William Livingston. William Living, The Independent Reflector-No. 46. Life and Letters of William Livingstone, reprinted by Theodore Sedgwick, Jr. Stephen Abbott Northrop, D.D., A Cloud of Witnesses (Portland, OR: American Heritage Ministries, 1987; Mantle Ministries, 228 Still Ridge, Bulverde, Texas), p. 288

[80] William Livingston. Livingston's Familiar Letters to a Gentleman, upon a variety of seasonable an important Subjects in Religion. Stephen Abbott Northrop, D.D., A Cloud of Witnesses (Portland, OR: American Heritage Ministries, 1987; Mantle Ministries, 228 Still Ridge, Bulverde, Texas), pp. 287-288

[81] James Madison. June 20, 1785. Robert Rutland, ed., The Papers of James Madison (Chicago: University of Chicago Press, 1973), Vol. VIII, pp. 299, 304

We have staked the whole future of American civilization, not upon the power of government, far from it. We have staked the future of all our political institutions upon the capacity of mankind for self-government; upon the capacity of each and all of us to govern ourselves, to control ourselves, to sustain ourselves according to the Ten Commandments of God.[82]

In a letter to Frederick Beasley on November 20, 1825, James Madison writes:

The belief in a God All Powerful wise and good, is so essential to the moral order of the World and to the happiness of man, that arguments which enforce it cannot be drawn from too many sources nor adapted with too much solicitude to the different characters and capacities to be impressed with it.[83]

George Mason

George Mason was very instrumental in the design of the Constitution but refused to sign it because he was a strong advocate of having a Bill of Rights go along with the original document to limit the power of the federal government. George Mason is called the Father of the Bill of Rights which was ratified two years after the Constitution.

In speaking before the General Court of Virginia, George Mason stated:

The laws of nature are the laws of God, whose authority can be superseded by no power on earth.[84]

George Mason who strongly disapproved of the slave trade stated during the debates of the Constitutional Convention:

Every master of slaves is born a petty tyrant. They bring the judgment of heaven upon a country. As nations cannot be

---

[82] James Madison. 1778. Frederick Nymeyer, Progressive Calvinism, (1958), Vol. 4 p. 31

[83] James Madison. November 20, 1825, in a letter to Frederick Beasley. A.D. Wainwright, ed., Madison and Witherspoon; Theological Roots of American Political Thought (The Princeton University Library Chronicle, Springs 1961), p. 125.

[84] George Mason. In an address before the General Court of Virginia. Russ Walton, Biblical Principles of Importance to Godly Christians (Marlborough, NH: The Plymouth rock foundation, 1984), p. 358

rewarded or punished in the next world, they must be in this. By an inevitable chain of causes and effects, Providence punishes national sins, by national calamities.[85]

Gouverneur Morris

Gouverneur Morris was the writer of the final draft of the Constitution. He spoke 173 times during the Constitutional debates which are the most of any other delegate. He wrote:

Religion is the only solid basis of good morals; therefore education should teach the precepts of religion, and the duties of man toward God.[86]

Thomas Paine

Thomas Paine signed neither the Declaration of Independence nor the Constitution of the United States but was very instrumental in helping prepare the hearts and minds of many Americans for the long Revolutionary battle ahead with his pamphlets called Common Sense. Excerpts from his writings include:

Tyranny, like hell, is not easily conquered; yet we have this consolation with us, that the harder the conflict, the more glorious the triumph. What we obtain too cheaply, we esteem too lightly; 'tis dearness only that gives everything its goods; and it would be strange indeed if so celestial an article as freedom should not be highly rated.[87]

The cause of America is in a great measure the cause of all mankind. Where, say some, is the king of America? I'll tell you, friend, He reigns above.[88]

The Almighty implanted in us these inextinguishable feeling for good and wise purposes. They are the guardians of His

---

[85] George Mason. August 22, 1787, in addressing the Continental Congress. James Madison, Notes of Debates in the Federal Convention of 1787 (1787, reprinted NY: W.W. Norton Co., 1987), p. 504

[86] Gouverneur Morris. Circa 1792, in "Notes of the Form for the King of France." Jared Sparks, ed., The Life of Gouverneur Morris, with Selections from His Correspondence and Miscellaneous Papers, 3 Vols. (Boston: Gray and Bowen 1832), Vol. III, p. 483

[87] Thomas Paine. December 23, 1776, in The American Crisis, No. 1 John Bartlett, Bartlett's Familiar Quotations (Boston: Little, Brown and Company, 1855, 1980), p. 384

[88] Thomas Paine. December 23, 1776. The American Crisis. "Common Sense" Thomas Paine—1776 (Reston, VA: Intercessors for America, July/August 1993), Vol. 20, No. 7/8, p. 1.

image in our heart. They distinguish us from the herd of common animals.[89]

Thomas Paine's last words were:

I die in perfect composure and resignation to the will of my Creator, God.[90]

Charles Cotesworth Pinckney

Charles Pinckney was a signer of the Constitution of the United States. He stated:

Blasphemy against the Almighty is denying His Being or Providence, or uttering contumelious reproaches on our Savior Christ. It is punished, at common law by fine and imprisonment, for Christianity is part of the laws of the land.[91]

And consequently, as man depends absolutely upon his Maker for everything, it is necessary that he should, in all points, conform to his Maker's will. This will of his Maker, is called the law of nature.[92]

Edmund Jennings Randolph

Edmund Randolph was a delegate at the Constitutional Convention but did not sign the Constitution. After Benjamin Franklin's famous address and appeal for prayer, Randolph further moved:

That a sermon be preached at the request of the convention on the 4th of July, the anniversary of Independence; &

---

[89] Thomas Paine. December 23, 1776. The American Crisis. "Common Sense" Thomas Paine—1776 (Reston, VA: Intercessors for America, July/August 1993), Vol. 20, No. 7/8, p. 1.

[90] Thomas Paine. The World Book Encyclopedia, 18 Vols. (Chicago, IL: Field Enterprises, Inc., 1957; W.F. Quarrie and Company, 8 Vols., 1917; World Book, Inc., 22 Vols., 1989), Vol. 13, p. 6035

[91] Charles Cotesworth Pinckney. Sir William Blackstone, Commentaries on the Laws of England (Philadelphia: J.B. Lippincott and Co., 1879), Vol. II, p. 59.

[92] Charles Cotesworth Pinckney. Sir William Blackstone, Commentaries on the Laws of England (Philadelphia: J.B. Lippincott and Co., 1879), Vol. I, p. 39.

thenceforward prayers be used in ye Convention every morning.[93]

Benjamin Rush

Benjamin Rush signed the Declaration of Independence. He co-founded the first American anti-slavery society. After the adoption of the Constitution he declared:

The only foundation for...a republic is to be laid in Religion. Without this there can be no virtue, and without virtue there can be no liberty, and liberty is the object and life of all republican governments.[94]

In writings published in 1798 he stated:

I know there is an objection among many people to teaching children doctrines of any kind, because they are liable to be controverted. But let us not be wiser than our Maker. If moral precepts alone could have reformed mankind, the mission of the Son of God into all the world would have been unnecessary. The perfect morality of the Gospels rests upon the doctrine which, though often controverted has never been refuted: I mean the vicarious life and death of the Son of God.[95]

Benjamin Rush described himself: *I have alternately been called an Aristocrat and a Democrat. I am neither. I am a Christocrat.*[96]

In writing to his wife before his death:

My excellent wife, I must leave you, but God will take care of you. By the mystery of Thy Holy incarnation; by Thy holy

---

[93] Edmund Jennings Randolph. June 28, 1787. James Madison, Notes of Debates in the Federal Convention of 1787 (1787; reprinted NY: W.W, Norton & Co., 1987; Mantle Ministries, 228 Still Ridge, Bulverde, Texas), pp. 373-374.

[94] Benjamin Rush. 1798. 1786, in "Thoughts upon the Mode of Education Proper in a Republic," published in Early American Imprints. Benjamin Rush, Essays, Literary, Moral and Philosophical, Philadelphia, 1798: "Of the Mode of Education Proper in a Republic." The Annals of America, 20 Vols. (Chicago, IL: Encyclopedia Britannica, 1968), Vol. 4. Pp. 28-29

[95] Benjamin Rush. Essays, Literary, Moral, and Philosophical (1798, 2nd edition, 1806). Stephen Abbott Northrop, D.D., A Cloud of Witnesses (Portland, OR: American Heritage Ministries, 1987; Mantle Ministries, 228 Still Ridge, Bulverde, Texas), p. 388

[96] Benjamin Rush. David Barton, Keys to Good Government (Aledo, TX: WallBuilder Press, 1994), p. 24

nativity; by Thy baptism, fasting, and temptation; by Thine agony and bloody sweat; by Thy cross and passion; by Thy precious death and burial; by Thy glorious resurrection and ascension, and by the coming of the Holy Ghost, blessed Jesus, wash away all my impurities, and receive me into Thy everlasting kingdom.[97]

Roger Sherman

Roger Sherman has the distinct honor of being the only Founder that signed all four major founding documents. He signed the Articles of Association in 1774 which was an agreement between the colonies on how to conduct themselves during their boycott of England after they'd raised taxes on the people. He signed the Declaration of Independence in 1776 and the Articles of Confederation in 1777 which was the original agreement between the states before the writing of the Constitution of the United States in 1787 which Roger Sherman also signed.

Roger Sherman was on a committee with John Adams and George Wythe to create instructions for the embassy in Canada. The instructions were as follows:

You are further to declare that we hold sacred the rights of conscience, and may promise to the whole people, solemnly in our name, the free and undisturbed exercise of their religion. And...that all civil rights and the right to hold office were to be extended to persons of any Christian denomination.[98]

In a speech, Roger Sherman discussed the importance of:

Admiring and thankfully acknowledging the riches of redeeming love, and earnestly imploring that divine

---

[97] Benjamin Rush. Essays, Literary, Moral, and Philosophical (1798, 2nd edition, 1806). Stephen Abbott Northrop, D.D., A Cloud of Witnesses (Portland, OR: American Heritage Ministries, 1987; Mantle Ministries, 228 Still Ridge, Bulverde, Texas), p. 388

[98] Roger Sherman. February 1776, in a directive for the embassy to Canada. Christopher Collier, Roger Sherman's Connecticut (Middletown, CT: Wesleyan University Press, 1979), p. 129

assistance which may enable us to live no more to ourselves, but to Him who loved us and gave Himself to die for us.[99]

Richard Stockton

Richard Stockton signed the Declaration of Independence. In his Will, Roger Stockton wrote:

> *As my children will have frequent occasion of perusing this instrument, and may probably be peculiarly impressed with the last words of their father, I think proper here, not only to subscribe to the entire belief of the great leading doctrine of the Christian religion... but also in the heart of a father's affection, to charge and exhort them to remember "that the fear of the Lord is the beginning of wisdom."*[100]

Noah Webster

Noah Webster did not sign either document but was a soldier in the Revolutionary War. He was largely responsible for Article I, Section 8 of the Constitution of the United States. He is also well known for writing Webster's dictionary. He wrote:

> *Education is useless without the Bible.*[101] He stated that *"The Bible was America's basic text book in all fields.*[102] And: *God's Word, contained in the Bible, has furnished all necessary rules to direct our conduct.*[103]

> Noah Webster wrote: *It is alleged by men of loose principles, or defective views of the subject, that religion and morality are not necessary or important qualifications for political stations. But the Scriptures teach a different doctrine. They direct that rulers should be men who rule in the fear of God, able men, such as fear God, men of truth, hating covetousness. But if we had no divine instruction on the subject, our own interest would demand of us a strict*

---

[99] Roger Sherman. John Eidsmoe, Constitution, p. 321
[100] Richard Stockton. In his Will. Edward J. Giddings, American Christian Rulers, p. 463
[101] Noah Webster. "Our Christian heritage," Letter from Plymouth rock (Marlborough, NH: The Plymouth Rock Foundation), p. 5
[102] Noah Webster. "Our Christian heritage," Letter from Plymouth rock (Marlborough, NH: The Plymouth Rock Foundation), p. 5
[103] Noah Webster. Verna M. Hall and Rosalie J. Slater, The Bible and the Constitution of the United States (San Francisco: Foundation for American Christian Education, 1983), p. 27

observance of the principle of these injunctions. And it is to the neglect of this rule of conduct in our citizens, that we must ascribe the multiplied frauds, breeches of trust, peculations and embezzlements of public property which astonish even ourselves; which tarnish the character of our country; which disgrace a republican government; and which will tend to reconcile men to monarchs in other countries and even our own.[104]

Webster wrote: *In my view, the Christian religion is the most important and one of the first things in which all children, under a free government ought to be instructed...No truth is more evident to my mind than that the Christian religion must be the basis of any government intended to secure the rights and privileges of a free people.[105]*

In a translation of the Bible, Noah prefaced it with:

The Bible is the Chief moral cause of all that is good, and the best corrector of all that is evil, in human society; the best for regulating the temporal concerns of men, and the only book that can serve as an infallible guide to future felicity...It is extremely important to our nation, in a political as well as a religious view, that all possible authority and influence should be given to the scriptures, for these furnish the best principles of civil liberty, and the most effectual support of republican government.

The principles of genuine liberty, and of wise laws and administrations, are to be drawn from the Bible and sustained by its authority. The man, therefore, who weakens or destroys the Divine authority of that Book may be accessory to all the public disorders which society is doomed to suffer...

There are two powers only, sufficient to control men and secure the rights of individuals and a peaceable

---

[104] Noah Webster. 1823, in his Letters to a Young Gentleman Commencing His Education (New Haven: Howe & Spalding, 1823), pp. 18-19.

[105] Noah Webster. 1828, in the preface to his American Dictionary of the English Language (reprinted San Francisco: Foundation for American Christian Education, 1967), Preface, p. 12

administration; these are the combined force of religion and law, and the force or fear of the bayonet.[106]

John Witherspoon

John Witherspoon was a signer of the Declaration of Independence, and in a speech, he declared: *"...Whoever is an avowed enemy of God, I scruple not to call him an enemy of his country."*[107]

Following his death, John Adams called John Witherspoon: *"A true son of liberty. So he was. But first, he was a son of the Cross."*[108]

These quotes are a small sampling of our Founding Fathers thoughts and beliefs. They each hold the God of the Universe and His Son Jesus in high regard. It's clear the Founders believed a republican form of government could not survive without people of virtue—a virtuous person by-definition conforms to moral and ethical principles. The definition of morals is applicable to actions that are good or evil, virtuous or vicious, and has reference to the law of God as the standard by which their character is to be determined (Webster's Dictionary, 1828). When we remove God from the picture and we look at a person with moral and ethical principles. We find according to political correctness; moral and ethical principles are simply what we want them to be. In other words, my moral and ethical principles can be radically different from yours. Take two main social issues of today, abortion or gay rights. God's word in the Bible is very clear about both issues. They are morally unacceptable. Today's society will say that both are morally acceptable. Without the foundation of God and His principles, people can and have made their own definition of what morality is.

The progressive movement eliminates any references to God for the Socialist movement to take hold. Morality according to God's principles, has no place in the progressive mindset. The

---

[106] Noah Webster. 1833. Noah Webster, Common Version of the Holy Bible, containing the Old and New Testament, with Amendments of the Language (1833), preface. Catherine Millard, The Rewriting of America's History (Camp Hill, PA: Horizon House Publishers, 1991), p. 160

[107] John Witherspoon. May 17, 1776, in his sermon entitled, "The Dominion of Providence over the Passions of Men" delivered at The College of New Jersey (Princeton). Barnum Lancing Collins, President Witherspoon (New York: Arno Press and The New York Times, 1969), I:197-98

[108] John Witherspoon. John Adams. Roger Schultz, "Covenanting in America: The Political Theology of John Witherspoon," Master's Thesis, Trinity Evangelical Divinity School, Deerfield, Illinois, 1985, p. 149

Founders and all moral individuals believe we received our rights from God and then we give power to the government to govern the people. All other forms of government, including ours 'today,' believe our rights come from the government, and they decide what powers to give us. With this philosophy, the government can take away our rights if they choose. Under the Founders plan, no one can take away our rights because they come from God. If you look at any Socialist/Communist country, God doesn't exist. Therefore, God and His principles must prevail if this republic is to survive. After the Revolutionary War, France tried to implement a similar type of constitution and government as America except they purposely left out the Divine Providence of God. It failed miserably.

Alexis de Tocqueville

Alexis de Tocqueville was a French jurist who visited the United States in 1831. Upon returning to France, he wrote a book called *Democracy in America*. Tocqueville writes:

> *On my arrival in the United States the religious aspect of the country was the first thing that struck my attention; and the longer I stayed there, the more I perceived the great political consequences resulting from this new state of things.*
> *In France I had almost always seen the spirit of religion and the spirit of freedom marching in opposite directions. But in America I found they were intimately united and that they reigned in common over the same country.[109]*

> He later continues: *Religion in America takes no direct part in the government of society, but it must be regarded as the first of their political institutions...I do not know whether all Americans have a sincere faith in their religion—for who can search the human heart? —but I am certain that they hold it to be indispensable to the maintenance of republican institutions. This opinion is not peculiar to a class of citizens or to a party, but it belongs to the whole nation and to every rank of society.[110]*

---

[109] Alexis de Tocqueville. Democracy in America (New York: Vintage Books, 1945), Vol. I, p. 319
[110] Alexis de Tocqueville. Democracy in America (New York: Vintage Books, 1945), Vol. I, p. 316

Continuing Tocqueville writes: *The sects* (referring to the different denominations of Christianity) *that exist in the United States are innumerable. They all differ in respect to the worship which is due to the Creator; but they all agree in respect to the duties which are due from man to man. Each sect adores the Deity in its own peculiar manner, but all sects preach the same moral law in the name of God...All the sects of the United States are comprised with the great unity of Christianity, and Christian morality is everywhere the same*[111]

...There is no country in the world where the Christian religion retains a greater influence over the souls of men then in America..."[112]

Continuing: *The revolutionists of America are obliged to profess an ostensible respect for Christian morality and equity, which does not permit them to violate wantonly the laws that opposed their designs...Thus, while the law permits the Americans to do what they please, religion prevents them from conceiving, and forbids them to commit, what is rash and unjust.*[113]

Later he writes about the schools in America*: In New England every citizen receives the elementary notions of human knowledge; he is taught, moreover, the doctrines and the evidences of his religion, the history of his country, and the leading features of its Constitution. In the states of Connecticut and Massachusetts, it is extremely rare to find a man imperfectly acquainted with all these things, and a person wholly ignorant of them is a sort of phenomenon.*[114]

Tocqueville spoke extensively about the clergy which wasn't included in this book, but I recommend you read.

One final quote from Tocqueville:

---

[111] Alexis de Tocqueville. Democracy in America (New York: Vintage Books, 1945), Vol. I, p. 303

[112] Alexis de Tocqueville. Democracy in America (New York: Vintage Books, 1945), Vol. I, p. 303

[113] Alexis de Tocqueville. Democracy in America (New York: Vintage Books, 1945), Vol. I, p. 316

[114] Alexis de Tocqueville. Democracy in America (New York: Vintage Books, 1945), Vol. I, p. 327

I sought for the greatness and genius of America in her commodious harbors and her ample rivers, and it was not there; in her fertile fields and boundless prairies, and it was not there; in her rich mines and her vast world commerce, and it was not there. Not until I went to the churches of America and heard her pulpits aflame with righteousness did I understand the secret of her genius and power. America is great because she is good, and if America ever ceases to be good, America will cease to be great.[115]

---

[115] Alexis de Tocqueville. Robert Flood, The Rebirth of America (The Arthur S. DeMoss Foundation, 1986), p. 32

Liberty Bell in Philadelphia, Pa.

Chapter 5

Freedom and Liberty

Noah Webster's 1828 dictionary describes

Freedom as: *A state of exemption from the power or control of another. Liberty; exemption from slavery, servitude or confinement.*

Liberty means: *Freedom from restraint, in a general sense, and applicable to the body, or to the will or mind.*

Paraphrasing: Freedom and liberty is the right to do what you want, with whom you want, for as long as you want assuming you have the means—without anyone telling you otherwise and assuming you're not infringing on someone else's freedom and liberty.

What does God say about freedom in the Bible? In Jeremiah (Old Testament, NIV), Chapter 34: God says:

"Recently you repented and did what is right in my sight: Each of you proclaimed freedom to your own people. You even made a covenant before me in the house that bears my Name".

In Psalm 119:45 NIV: *"I will walk about in freedom, for I have sought out your precepts."* Where 'precepts' means

(Webster's 1828): *Any commandment or order intended as an authoritative rule of action; but applied particularly to commands respecting moral conduct.*

In 2 Corinthians 3:17 NIV Paul writes: *"Now the Lord is the Spirit, and where the Spirit of the Lord is, there is freedom."*

In 1 Peter 2:16 NIV, Peter writes: *"Live as free people, but do not use your freedom as a cover-up for evil; live as God's slaves."*

In Galatians 5:13 NIV: *"You, my brothers and sisters, were called to be free. But do not use your freedom to indulge the flesh; rather, serve one another humbly in love."*

The Bible is filled with scripture that speaks of freedom but let's end with this one:

John 8:32 NIV: *"Then you will know the truth, and the truth will set you free."*

Have you given any thought to what freedom means to you? As a Christian, you've been set free by the power of the Holy Spirit. If you're an American, you have been set free by God through the Declaration of Independence and the Constitution of the United States of America. This means the government has no authority to take away our freedom without our consent. Unfortunately, Washington, D.C. has been "assuming consent" and usurping our freedom with little or no resistance from the people.

One example of this is the "vapor cigarette businesses." A relatively new business on the market that was growing at a rapid rate until the FDA stepped in to place serious regulations on them. They require vapor companies to follow the same strict regulations of the tobacco companies. Not to argue whether they were warranted or not but to say, these regulations will shut down most of the businesses because only the tobacco companies could afford these new regulations. Fortunately for the vapor business, as of early 2017, the FDA has decided to postpone the new rules.

Hundreds of years before the official founding of our nation, people came to this land to start over and be free to worship God as they were led to do. They didn't want to follow a government-sponsored religion. They wanted a God sponsored relationship. When people are released from the bondage of sin and a repressive government, our minds are free to look at the possibilities of life. We are free to look at what things can be like instead of the way things are. We can DREAM.

Today many Americans have lost the ability to dream of a better lifestyle, a better education, a better marriage. Many have lost the desire for their children to live better lives than they did. Having no real goals or dreams, they show up at work just to 'get through the day.' Go home and have a few drinks, go to bed just to do it all over again tomorrow. This brings complacency, bitterness, laziness and ultimately back into bondage. Since they've lost their desire to dream big how can they teach their children to dream big? If they don't teach their children how to dream big, then evil will prevail.

Progressives will promise to give us things that may make our lives better without the work it takes to acquire it ourselves—which leads further into a life of dependency. With an attitude of dependency, we are persuaded by the next best politician who "feels our pain,"—claiming to help but actually seeing an opportunity to gain more power, control, and money. They take advantage of people who've lost their souls and are looking for a savior to rescue them.

Freedom is being able to walk away from a high paying job to write a book—one that will make a difference in people's lives. It's giving up the security of a job to do something they believe can make the country a better place to live—while at the same time promising your wife of thirty-three plus years of marriage everything will be ok. Freedom is having faith in a Power greater than I and knowing at the core of my being He's in control. Freedom is knowing my four adult children are watching me and believing in me to succeed—counting on me to set an example for them and their children. Freedom is realizing you could fail and fall flat on your face—but knowing you have the choice to get back up and go again. Freedom is knowing no matter how many times you fail, by getting back up you win. Can you say that in other countries? Perhaps you can today, but ONLY because America set a notable example for other countries to follow. Regardless of what some politicians say, we are an EXCEPTIONAL country. We have made many mistakes—but we keep getting back up to fight another day.

The Free Enterprise System

The free enterprise system in America is the greatest system ever devised by mankind—despite the common misconception that's permeated throughout the land. ANYONE no matter what their challenges are in life can DECIDE not to let it affect them and their goals.

Stories have been told about people with major disabilities achieving success...people with very dark backgrounds, turning things around and achieving success...people from incredibly low levels of poverty coming out and making it big...people who repeatedly failed, eventually succeeding. It's simply a mindset that, in America, we refuse to allow our position in life to keep us from achieving our dreams.

America doesn't have the largest land mass, the greatest number of people or the most natural resources. We haven't been around the longest; don't have the best schools or even the smartest people. We didn't start with the most money or the biggest and best military. So, what made us so GREAT?

The free enterprise system (capitalism) made us great. It's an economic system in which investment in, and ownership of, the means of production, distribution, and exchange of wealth is made and maintained chiefly by private individuals or corporations.[116] It's a system that allows a person to own property. If he works hard and smart, he can gain more property. If he chooses not to work hard and smart, there will be no gain. It's his or her choice.

The Founders believed in allowing Americans the opportunity to "pursue happiness." They were aware, and so are we, that money can't buy happiness. Money is generally a bi-product of what created our happiness. If you've created a successful business, your happiness is derived from the accomplishment of your work, not the money you earned. If you finished a doctorate and now working in medicine, your happiness is in helping people with health issues or proactively keeping people healthy. The money you earn isn't what's making you happy. Happiness and success come from pleasing your

---

[116] Random House College Dictionary (New York) 1981

customers and patients not by donating to the government or politicians.

If your parents give you money when you are a child, or the government gives you money from welfare, or you win the lottery—you're excited until the money runs out. You then want more and won't be happy until it's provided for you. This is one of many reasons why socialism will never work. Creating or working for your money generates a strong moral character deep in your spirit. Unearned wealth will eventually destroy any moral character you have.

Why then, is the desire for socialism growing so rapidly in this country? …Because professors and teachers are promoting progressivism in school. Socialism keeps everyone equal except for the elite which becomes extremely rich. By keeping everyone equal, means equally poor. You cannot get rich in the socialistic system because the government owns the property, production, and financial growth (if any). Therefore, there's no reason to dream big, work hard, or strive for more. Your incentive for success is removed. Socialism only benefits the elite and the lazy. Study any socialistic/communistic country today, or in history will prove the point. Don't believe the argument that we can do it better or do it right in America. That's a lie from hell. Any true success in life is based on solid fundamental principles—which socialism lacks. Just look at Venezuela for recent proof that socialism leads to destruction. Progressives will distort the truth and say that they didn't do it right. No…they did it exactly right, and it proved a total failure.

If you have a dream, challenge yourself to be successful. Put God and your family as the benefactors of your dreams. Hold yourself accountable and don't let anyone tell you that you can't have your dreams. Don't worry about failure; it's only temporary. Get back up and go again. It's not about wishing and hoping; it's about striving and succeeding. Plenty of people will try to hold you back—but freedom is about making a choice to succeed. The free enterprise system is for people who want a better life for themselves, their family and their country.

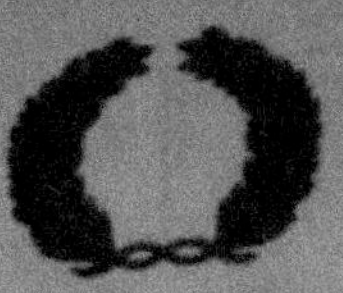

Inscription on the wall of the Jefferson Memorial

Chapter 6

Creator and the Creation

John Locke was an English philosopher and physician who lived during the 1600s and was highly regarded by our Founders. The Founders quoted John Locke on many occasions. They agreed with his understanding and philosophy of who the Creator is. Locke describes an atheist as someone who's decided not to address the possibility of a Creator—he's out of touch with reality and irrational. God has made Himself obvious and recognizable. Locke says—an atheist has failed to apply his divine capacity for reason and observation. The Founding Fathers agreed with Locke in that these were self-evident truths—paraphrasing, Locke explains: to think for a moment that the world, just out of coincidence could possibly form as it has is absurd...Or the human eye or ear, with all its intricacies, could form on its own, not happening. From John Locke's essay called "Concerning Human Understanding"[117]

Natural Law and Natural Rights

The definitions, natural law or laws of nature are the same. In the American Dictionary of the English Language by Noah Webster (1828), the law of nature is defined as follows: a rule of conduct arising out of the natural relations of human beings

---

[117] Great Books of the Western World, vol. 35, Encyclopedia Britannica, Inc., Chicago, 1952, pp. 349-352

established by the Creator, and existing prior to any positive precept. Thus, it is a law of nature, that one man should not injure another, and murder and fraud would be crimes, independent of any prohibition from a supreme power.

Moral Law is defined as a law which prescribes to men their religious and social duties, their duties to God and to each other. The moral law is summarily contained in the Decalogue or Ten Commandments, written by the finger of God on two tables of stone, and delivered to Moses on Mount Sinai (Webster's 1828 dictionary).

The Framers read, studied and often quoted John Locke, William Blackstone, Plato, Aristotle, and Marcus Cicero just to name a few. Both Plato and Aristotle spoke of natural law; it was Marcus Cicero that best explains what the philosophy of natural law is. The Founders leaned heavily on his interpretation of natural law. Understanding Cicero called natural law as "true law," he said:

> *"True law is right reason in agreement with nature; it is of universal application, unchanging and everlasting; it summons to duty by its commands and averts from wrongdoing by its prohibitions...It is a sin to try to alter this law, nor is it allowable to repeal any part of it, and it is impossible to abolish it entirely. We cannot be freed from its obligations by senate or people, and we need not look outside ourselves for expounder or interpreter of it. And there will not be different laws at Rome and Athens, or different laws now and in the future, but one eternal and unchangeable law will be valid for all nations and all times, and there will be one master and ruler, that is God, over us all, for he is the author of this law, its promulgator, and tis enforcing judge. Whoever is disobedient is fleeing from himself and denying his human nature, and by reason of this very fact he will suffer the worst punishment."[118]*

Cicero, who died in 43 B.C., studied Aristotle and Plato's writings. In evaluating our mental processes, Cicero's philosophy was that

---

[118] Ebenstein, W. (1956). Great Political Thinkers: Plato to the Present. The Western Political Quarterly, 9(4), 133. doi:10.2307/444535

this was a special, divine endowment from our Creator... Cicero wrote:

> *"The animal which we call man, endowed with foresight and quick intelligence, complex, keen, possessing memory, full of reason and prudence, has been given a certain distinguished status by the Supreme God who created him; for he is the only one among so many different kinds and varieties of living beings who has a share in reason and thought, while all the rest are deprived of it. But what is more divine, I will not say in man only, but in all heaven and earth, than reason? And reason, when it is full grown and perfected, is rightly called wisdom. Therefore, since there is nothing better than reason, and since it exists both in man and God, the first common possession of man and God is reason."*[119]

Cicero continues: *"But those who have reason in common must also have right reason in common. And since right reason is law we must believe who share Law must also share Justice; and those who share these are to be regarded as members of the same commonwealth. If indeed they obey the same authorities and powers, this is true in a far greater degree; but as a matter of fact, they do obey this celestial system, the divine mind, and the God of transcendent power. Hence, we must now conceive of this whole universe as one commonwealth of which both gods and men are members."*[120]

In the book of Matthew 22:36-40, Jesus was teaching in the public square, and the crowds were astonished by His teachings. The Pharisees and the Sadducees were not happy that Jesus was strongly influencing the people. They conspired to discredit Jesus by asking a question they believed would trip Jesus up and embarrass Him in front of all the people.

The Scripture reads: *"Teacher, which is the greatest commandment in the Law?" Jesus replied: 'Love the Lord*

---

[119] Ebenstein, W. (1969). Great Political Thinkers: Plato to the present. New York: Holt, Rinehart and Winston.

[120] Ebenstein, W. (1969). Great Political Thinkers: Plato to the present. New York: Holt, Rinehart and Winston.

your God with all your heart and with all your soul and with all your mind.' This is the first and greatest commandment. And the second is like it: 'Love your neighbor as yourself.' All the Law and the Prophets hang on these two commandments."

With this said, what is 'natural law'? Natural Law, like gravity, can't be seen, but you know it's there. Natural Law is laws designed by our Creator, God, which is absolute law. They cannot be changed or altered. The Founders believe that our natural rights (Unalienable Rights) extended from natural law. Since God designed natural laws, He then extends unalienable rights directly from the natural laws. Therefore, what God has given us, no man or government can take away.

John Locke wrote: *"The state of nature has a law of nature to govern it, which…teaches all mankind who will but consult it, that being all equal and independent, no one ought to harm another in his life, health, liberty or possessions; for men being all the workmanship of one omnipotent and infinitely wise maker; all the servants of one sovereign master, sent into the world by his order and about His business; they are His property…"*[121]

The following are some principles derived from our natural laws:
- Unalienable rights
- Habeas corpus
- Limited government
- Separation of powers
- Checks and balances
- Self-preservation

These are examples of the unalienable rights given to us by our Creator:
- Right to bear arms
- Self-government
- Own property
- Assemble
- Petition

---

[121] Locke, J. (2011). Second treatise of government. Hamburg, Germany: Tredition.

- Free speech
- Privacy

The Declaration of Independence is the 'outline' for the Constitution of the United States. The Declaration of Independence references these natural rights, natural laws and the Creator who gave them to us. The Constitution places the laws in place to protect our rights. Hence, these are critical ties between the two documents.

Separation of Powers and Checks and Balances

Political philosophers have been writing about the design of the perfect government long before the birth of Jesus. Polybius was a Greek who lived 204 to 122 B.C. When Rome conquered Greece, he was deported to Rome.

While studying different forms of governments, Polybius was the first to write about combining three key elements of governments, into one constitution. He envisioned an executive, senate and the people's assembly. He felt this would counter-balance one another thereby having no one power dominate the other, in turn protecting the people. He later died, and nothing came of it.

During the mid-1700s, Charles de Montesquieu, from France studied abroad and wrote a book utilizing the 3-branch idea only combining the Senate and the people's assembly into one branch and adding the judicial branch. Obviously, the Founders admired this idea and enacted it for the first time in history.

John Adams pushed the idea of the three separate powers idea from Montesquieu without much support from anyone else. Over time and much debate, this form was recognized by the Congress and put into place.

James Madison said the trick was to separate the three powers and then delicately lace them back together again as a balanced unit. Federalist Papers No. 47-51 discuss this in great detail. In Federalist No. 51 James Madison writes:

"In framing a government which is to be administered by men over men, the difficulty lies in this: you must first enable the government to control the governed; and in the next place oblige it to control itself. A dependence on the people is, no doubt, the primary control on the government; but experience has taught mankind the necessity of auxiliary precautions."

There were two major challenges with a republican style government:

- Democratic tyranny: the abuse of the minority or individual rights by an overbearing majority.
- Democratic ineptitude: the problem of making a democratic form of government efficient and effective.

The Founders wanted the power of the government divided amongst three different divisions to reduce the ability of the government to become too powerful; therefore eradicating the liberty of the people by becoming a tyrannical government. Madison wrote in Federalist Papers No. 47:

"...the preservation of liberty requires that the three great departments of power should be separate and distinct...The accumulation of all powers, legislative, executive, and judiciary, in the same hands whether of one, a few, or many, and whether hereditary, self-appointed, or elective, may justly be pronounced the very definition of tyranny."

In Federalist Papers No. 51, Madison explains how this structure of government forces the powers to work together for the liberty of the people and makes it difficult for tyranny to develop.

"The great security against a gradual concentration of the several powers in the same department consists in giving to those who administer each department the necessary constitutional means and personal motives to resist encroachments of the others."

The Founders concern at the Constitutional Convention was the fear or tendency toward a single centralized and all-powerful national government. In Federalist No. 39, Madison said that *"neither wholly federal nor wholly national"* government but a composite of the two, an incomplete national government.

In studying the intent of the Founders, it's completely obvious the Framers did everything they could to limit the possibility of the federal government becoming too powerful. They knew if this happened, they'd usurped the power from the states and the people would lose their liberty. Remember, our rights are given to us by God Himself. Therefore, the government has no authority to usurp (take away) our rights.

Virtue and Virtuous

Webster's 1828 dictionary says: Virtue is moral goodness; the practice of moral duties and the abstaining from vice, or conformity of life and conversation to the moral law. The practice of moral duties from sincere love to God and his laws is virtue and religion. Virtue is voluntary obedience to the truth.

Samuel Adams points out the importance of us electing virtuous people stating:

> *"But neither the wisest Constitution nor the wisest laws will secure the liberty and happiness of a people whose manners are universally corrupt. He, therefore, is the truest friend to the liberty of his country who tries most to promote its virtue, and who, so far as his power and influence extend, will not suffer a man to be chosen into any office of power and trust who is not a wise and virtuous man."*[122]

Scripture backs this theory up very well: Exodus 18:21 *But select capable men from all the people—men who fear God, trustworthy men who hate dishonest gain—and appoint them as officials over thousands, hundreds, fifties and tens.* Also, Proverbs 29:2 which states: *When the righteous thrive, the people rejoice; when the wicked rule, the people groan.*

Property Rights

---

[122] Wells, Life of Samuel Adams,1:22.

The unalienable right to own property is addressed in the Declaration of Independence and protected by the Constitution. Americans are afforded the right to work hard and earn money to purchase land and property in this country. The Founders used the term "industrious people" and "industry" when referring to our desire and ability to work hard to acquire property.

Noah Webster's 1828 dictionary describes "industry" this way: *"Habitual diligence in any employment, either bodily or mental; steady attention to business; assiduity; opposed to sloth and idleness. We are directed to take lessons of industry from the bee. Industry pays debts, while idleness or despair will increase them."*

Across the ocean, land was acquired by force, conquest, and violence for thousands of years and in some cases, still happening. The land then belonged to the new king or government. In America, we fought wars for the land as well but afterward, the land was generally distributed to the people. At which point the government would protect our right to continue to own the land until we sold it or lost it for legal reasons.

As the population of America expanded, the land was distributed. Eventually, there wasn't any additional property to give away. Thomas Jefferson knew there's no tangible way to distribute the land in a fair and balances way. Land, once given, belonged to the family and the Constitution protects posterity. Jefferson wrote:

> *"I am conscious that an equal division of property is impracticable, but the consequences of this enormous inequality producing so much misery to the bulk of mankind, legislators cannot invent too many devices for subdividing property, only taking care to let their subdivisions go hand in hand with the natural affections of the human mind."*

When an immigrant came to America with his family and little money—it was their responsibility to work hard (be industrious) and save what they could. Over time, they would save enough money to purchase their own property. This property remained in their family while the next generation worked hard, saved and expanded their land. Gradually and with the proper industrious spirit prevalent in the family, they became 'the rich.'

This is the beauty of being free and able to own property while utilizing the free enterprise system.

If we weren't allowed to own property, what incentive would we have to become industrious? We'd have no need to work hard to earn anything but our family's daily needs, such as food, clothing and a roof over our heads to protect us from the weather. There would be no incentive to go out and create — no reason to strive to better ourselves or our families.

Having the ability to own property—and the government obligated to protect our property offers incentives to be industrious. Without this protection, we would face internal fights and wars because protecting our property would be our own responsibility. The poor and weak would always be on the losing end of that fight. Jefferson wrote: *The "first principle of association is the guarantee to everyone the free exercise of his industry and the fruits acquired by it."*[123]

When the progressive movement began, government hostility toward owning property grew at a steady rate. Owning property is unacceptable to the progressives because it becomes an unfair advantage for one person over another. By denying God's presence at the founding of the nation, they can argue unalienable rights do not exist which is an important reason they rebuke the existence of God. If God doesn't exist, then there's no unalienable rights and no right to own property.

In the book of Numbers, chapters 34 thru 36, God explains to Moses and the Israelites how the land will be distributed. He also clarifies how the land is to be passed down to seceding generations within the family. God intended for man to own land 4000 years ago and still does to this day.

Next, the progressives don't agree that owning property was an adequate way to promote economic growth. They claim the government is responsible for expanding growth to the economy.

Lastly, progressives believe that owning property corrupts people and holds the poor down. Again, this is another distortion of the truth. Refer to the example of an immigrant coming to the

---

[123] Letter to Milligan, 6 April 1816, in Writings of Thomas Jefferson, ed. Albert E. Bergh (Washington: Thomas Jefferson Memorial Association, 1904, 14:466

country with no money and become extremely successful. It's not luck, its industry.

With the vast amount of progressive changes that have occurred over the last 120 plus years, where is God now in all this? Why has He allowed America to fall so far to the left of center in our political perspective? With God's involvement at the beginning, is He still involved today?

People ask: where is God during the school shootings; where is He during the bar shootings, church shootings or the Las Vegas shootings? Why has He allowed all this to happen as well?

I would argue that God is still engaged but "We the People" have disengaged in the process. We have kicked God out of the schools. We have kicked God out of our political process. Just pull up the YouTube video of the 2012 Democratic National Convention, and you'll see how desperately hard one of the leaders worked to return God in. He's no longer allowed in the public square.

God is in control, but He does allow us the free-will to make our own decisions. We started disengaging in the early 1900s with Woodrow Wilson and Teddy Roosevelt impacting the Constitution and gave power to the Administrative State. We disengaged when we allowed Franklin D. Roosevelt to install the "New Deals" during the 1930s...Then eight years of Barack Obama where we were disengaged and allowed him to pass laws utilizing executive orders and administrative regulations.

So where is God in all this? I'd argue that President Obama, like King Sol of Israel were wake-up calls. God ordained both Obama and Sol, and they were well-liked, by the people. But they each pushed the limits of their position waking people up to re-engaging in the process. And knowing how close Hillary Clinton was to following President Obama scared a multitude of people.

So where is God when it comes to President Trump. First-off, I'm not sure there is a man alive today that could withstand the abuse President Trump has had to overcome—both from inside his party as well as outside. Here is a man that truly didn't need the job or the abuse. Yet took on the challenge and won. In less than two years, President Trump has:

- ■ Set Jerusalem as the location of our American Embassy despite world opposition.

- Sided with Israel on numerous issues that President Obama opposed.
- Has put Christ back into our Christmas holiday
- Chose pro-life Constitutionalist Judges for the Supreme Court
- Chose a God-Fearing Vice President in VP Mike Pence
- Appointed a U.N. Ambassador, that's turned the United Nations on its head
- Eliminated many if not all the Obama Executive Orders that have stifled American business
- Lowered taxes allowing the American people to keep more of their money
- Worked harder to protect our land borders than any recent President
- Is building a wall on our southern border in spite of the overwhelming opposition

You can decide whether a Trump Presidency was from God engaging on our behalf or not but from what I've seen thus far—I'd say, 'obviously yes.'

Foundering Fathers during the Constitutional Convention

Chapter 7

A Country Divided

Currently, America is divided—and not since the Civil War in the mid-1800s have we been this divided. Could this be a natural cycle that an empire goes through?

Our national pledge says it all: "One nation under God, indivisible." We are a nation rejecting God, and we've been divided. This was an organized plan from the progressives which require division to succeed—and they've succeeded. Here are some of the ways:

- Whites vs. Blacks
- Rich vs. the Poor
- Old vs. the Young
- Conservatives vs. the Liberals
- Republicans vs. the Democrats
- Middle America vs. the Coast
- Elites vs. Common Folks
- Judicial system vs. the Executive Branch

How did we get so divided as a nation? The answer—the progressive movement has taken over both political parties, our media, and our educational system.

The Founder believed we must teach our children about the Constitution and the Bible. We must understand where we began so we don't fall into the trap we're in now.

There's a classic saying: "Never talk about Politics and Religion." Since there are no two subjects that affect our everyday lives more than politics and religion, why wouldn't we talk about them—they'd certainly create a lively debate? A good honest and respectful debate will keep you well informed and curious at the same time.

Unfortunately, today people do talk about both subjects—only in heated discussions in which neither side will bend. The sad thing is there's so much miss-information (or fake news) being spread that it's difficult to know the difference between the truth and a lie—arguably, confusion being another tool of the progressives.

Looking at the two definitions for politics and religion we find the following:

- The modern-day definition of politics from Merriam-Webster (last updated on 31 December 2017), a) the art or science of government; b) the art or science concerned with guiding or influencing governmental policy; c) the art or science concerned with winning and holding control over a government.

- The modern-day definition of religion from Merriam-Webster (last updated on 16 Dec 2017) lists four definitions. Here are 2 of the 4... The first is the service and worship of God or the supernatural—commitment or devotion to religious faith or observance. And the second is a cause, principle, or system of beliefs held to with ardor (enthusiasm or passion) and faith.

Based on the above definitions everyone has a religion. You may believe in the Judeo-Christian God, Mohammed's god, the Greek gods, etc. Or perhaps your passion and enthusiasm lead you to believe in the religion of evolution, mother-nature, climate change, atheism or the next best thing that comes along. Your religious beliefs control your thoughts and analysis of the data presented to you.

Therefore, when you try to determine where you stand on a political issue, the overwhelming guiding criteria to your decisions must be based on where you stand with your religious beliefs. You can't separate the two. Religion and politics go together.

So, when the atheists argued to the Supreme Court that we must have a "separation of church and state" they were saying that America must change from the Founder's religious belief of Christianity to his religious belief of atheism.

By making this change, we relinquish our 'Godly based moral standards' that doesn't change and has stood the test of time—to a moral standard that depends solely on the individual's personal feelings at any given time. Where one's personal feelings may supersede another person's feelings, based on the strength of their political influence. Politics and religion cannot be separated. This explains why the Founders believed that if you take Christianity out of the republican form of government, it cannot survive. October 11, 1798, John Adams wrote:

> *"We have no government armed with power capable of contending with human passions unbridled by morality and religion. Avarice, ambition, revenge, or gallantry, would break the strongest cords of our Constitution as a whale goes through a net. Our Constitution was made only for a moral and religious people. It is wholly inadequate to the government of any other."*[124]

Looking at the corruption and lack of accountability in Washington today, it's obvious the Founders were correct.

Poverty and Welfare

Over the last 100 years, progressivism has taught students that the Founders had no compassion for the poor and needy. This is far from the truth. The Founders believed we must help the poor and needy get back on their feet. They felt it should be taken care of by the tithes of the community churches, local businesses

---

[124] Adams, John. (Oct.11, 1798), Letter to the Massachusetts Militia

and the local government itself. The philosophy behind this is for the community to have a vested interest in its citizens—contributing to the success of the whole community. Secondly, the community would know the actual situation of the people and are in a better position to decide how best to deal with it—was it a health problem, down on their luck or they just didn't want to work. This would help prevent or reduce abuses and freeloading.

Liberty is critical to the success of the nation. If the federal government plays a very small role in the lives of every American, then churches could prosper and help the needy. The Founders were totally against redistribution of wealth by taking from the producers and giving to the non-producers. Jefferson wrote:

> *To take from one, because it is thought his own industry and that of his fathers has acquired too much, in order to spare to others, who, or whose fathers, have not exercised equal industry and skill, is to violate arbitrarily the first principle of association (the right to liberty), the guarantee to everyone the free exercise of his industry and the fruits acquired by it[125].*

Any laws written by the community to support the poor were not intended to go beyond a minimal safety net. Benefit levels were low to discourage people from not working. The Founders believed the main remedy for poverty, in a land of opportunity, was marriage and work.

Ben Franklin, while living in England in 1760, witnessed the government of Great Britain giving the poor an incentive not to become self-supporting. The poor were given enough that they could live in idleness. The result of this was increased poverty. Franklin wrote:

> *"I am for doing good to the poor, but I differ in opinion of the means. I think the best way of doing good to the poor, is not making them easy in poverty, but leading or driving them out of it. In my youth I traveled much, and I observed in different countries, that the more public provisions were made for the poor, the less they provided for themselves, and*

---

125 Thomas Jefferson, letter to Milligan, 6 April 1816, in Writings of Thomas Jefferson, ed. Albert E. Bergh (Washington: Thomas Jefferson Memorial Association, 1904), 14:466

of course became poorer. And, on the contrary, the less was done for them, the more they did for themselves, and became richer. There is no country in the world where so many provisions are established for them than England ...with a solemn general law made by the rich to subject their estates to a heavy tax for the support of the poor... Yet there is no country in the world in which the poor are more idle, dissolute, drunken, and insolent. The day you Englishmen passed that act, you took away from before their eyes the greatest of all inducements to industry, frugality, and sobriety, by giving them a dependence on somewhat else than a careful accumulation during youth and health for support in age and sickness. In short, you offered a premium for the encouragement of idleness, and you should not now wonder that it has had its effect in the increase of poverty."[126]

You could say Ben Franklin was prophetic when he wrote this statement because America has fallen into the same situation. The people living in poverty in America would be considered very rich in other countries. When in Nicaragua almost three years ago, the missionary said the average income for each citizen was two dollars per day. Children had no toys whatsoever, and families live in little one-room shacks with one bed if they were lucky. The dogs, cats, and cattle were thin as rails, hardly any meat on their bones—and we were informed not to give any food to the animals because the people didn't have enough food for themselves.

In America, our poor have cell phones, enough money to get by without getting a job if they choose not to, enough food stamps to buy steaks, lobsters and plenty of junk food. Working in the grocery business for 30 years will open your eyes to the disservice we do to our poor by removing any incentive to succeed. On numerous occasions, many of my employees have turned down extra hours because they didn't want to lose their welfare. That's not their fault; it's our government's fault for giving our poor NO incentive to get out of their situation. Again, this is also by design of the progressives to keep people poor and

---

[126] (Benjamin Franklin, "On the Price of Corn, and Management of the Poor" London Chronicle (November 1766), in Writings, ed. J.A. Leo Lemay (New York: Library of America, 1987), 587-88)

dependent on the government, to continue to stay in power by receiving their vote.

Franklin pointed out, when we remove the incentive for people to become industrious, they will remain poor and fall further into poverty. Progressives desire to keep as many people in poverty as possible and continue to support them with the minimal amount of funds to obtain their vote and stay in power. Almost, without exception, look at any of America's long term Democratically (progressive) controlled cities, you will find the highest rate of poverty and crime—which is by design and purposefully implemented.

Slavery

Noah Webster's 1828[127] definitions:

Slave: *A person who is wholly subject to the will of another; one, who has no will of his own, but whose person and services are wholly under the control of another.*

Slavery: *Bondage; the state of entire subjection of one person to the will of another. Slavery is the obligation to labor for the benefit of the master, without the contract or consent of the servant. Slavery may proceed from crimes, from captivity or from debt. Slavery is also voluntary or involuntary; slavery no longer exists in Great Britain, nor in the northern states of America.*

Slavery was a dark part of America's history—something we wish never happened. Unfortunately, slavery did occur, and we can't hide from it either. In today's unstable environment this topic makes people uncomfortable but needs to be addressed.

Slavery didn't originate in America. In researching the topic, the Holy Bible speaks of slaves or slavery nearly 200 times—going as far back in ancient times as the ninth chapter in the first book. The book of Genesis references slavery 25 times. Since then, slavery has been utilized by empires and governments for thousands of years—enslaving any race or religion. With that

---

[127] Webster, N. (1995). An American dictionary of the English language: an introductory dissertation of the origin, history and connection of the language of Western Asia, and of Europe and a concise grammar of the English language. San Francisco, CA: The Foundation for American Christian Education.

said, American slavery was about African Americans, so we'll start there.

In the early 1400s, a Portuguese exploration of the African coastline came upon a country of Arabs utilizing African slaves to mine their products. This explorer recognized an opportunity to use slaves in their sugar groves, so he began purchasing slaves and brought them back to Portugal. Soon this practice began to grow. In 1452, Pope Nicholas V issued a decree granting the right to enslave any non-Catholic believer into slavery which legitimized the slave trade under Catholic beliefs of that time[128]. With the Pope's endorsement, slavery spread throughout Europe.

Forty years later Christopher Columbus sailed the ocean for the Indi's. Upon discovery of a new world, word spread quickly about this new land. With many of the Colonies being from Europe, the Europeans brought their culture of slavery with them to America.

Fast forward three hundred years later in America, the slave trade had become a major 'industry' of the American lifestyle. Then in 1776, fifty-six men signed a Declaration of Independence stating that "All people are created equal." They did not say all white people are created equal, but 'All' people are created equal. This became the beginning of the end of slavery around the world.

At the signing of the Declaration of Independence, all thirteen states had been utilizing slavery. By the end of the founding era, seven of the thirteen states had passed laws forbidding slavery. And every prominent Founder is on record saying slavery was wrong. Here are a few examples:

George Washington stated: *"There is not a man living who wishes more sincerely than I do, to see a plan adopted for the abolition of it."*[129]

John Adams states: *"Every measure of prudence, therefore, ought to be assumed for the eventual total extirpation of slavery*

---

[128] Pope Nicolas V and the Portuguese Slave Trade · African Laborers for a New Empire: Iberia, Slavery, and the Atlantic World · Lowcountry Digital History Initiative. (n.d.). Retrieved February 20, 2018, from http://ldhi.library.cofc.edu/exhibits/show/african_laborers_for_a_new_emp/pope_nicolas_v_and_th e_portugu

[129] George Washington to Morris, 12 April 1786, in George Washington: A Collection, ed. W.B. Allen (Indianapolis: Liberty Classics, 1989), 319

from the United States...I have, through my whole life, held the practice of slavery in...abhorrence."[130]

Ben Franklin states: *"Slavery is ...an atrocious debasement of human nature.[131]"*

Alexander Hamilton states: *"The laws of certain states...give an ownership in the service of Negroes as personal property...But being men, by the laws of God and nature, they were capable of acquiring liberty—and when the captor in war...thought fit to give them liberty, the gift was not only valid, but irrevocable."[132]*

James Madison: *"We have seen the mere distinction of color made in the most enlightened period of time, a ground of the most oppressive dominion ever exercised by man over man."[133]*

John Jay stated: *"That men should pray and fight for their own freedom and yet keep others in slavery is certainly acting a very inconsistent as well as unjust and perhaps impious part."[134]*

James Otis from the Massachusetts legislature, in 1764 stated: *"The colonists are by the law of nature freeborn, as indeed all men are, white or black."[135]*

House of Representatives of New York: In 1776, stated that slavery is *"utterly inconsistent with the avowed principles in which this and other states have carried on their struggle for liberty."[136]*

The Founders believed slavery had to end—and worked hard to rectify the practice. This was a blemish on our past which

---

[130] John Adams to Evans, 8 June 1819, in Selected Writings of John and John Quincy Adams, ed. Adrienne Koch and William Peden (New York: Knopf, 1946), 209.

[131] Benjamin Franklin, "An Address to the Public from the Pennsylvania Society for Promoting the Abolition of Slavery" (1789), in Writings, ed. J.A. Leo Lemay (New York: Library of America, 1987), 1154.

[132] Hamilton, Philo Camillus No.2 (1795), in Papers of Alexander Hamilton, ed. Harold C. Syrett (New York: Columbia University Press, 1961-79), 19:101-2

[133] James Madison, speech at Constitutional Convention, 6 June 1787, in The Records of the Federal Convention of 1787, ed. Max Farrand (New Haven: Yale University Press, 1937), 1:135.

[134] Jay to Price, 27 September 1785, in Founders' Constitution, ed. Kurland and Lerner, 1:538

[135] James Otis, The Rights of the British Colonies (1764), in Pamphlets of the American Revolution, id. Bernard Bailyn (Cambridge: Harvard University Press, 1965), 1:439.

[136] Leon F. Litwack, North of Slavery: The Negro in the Free States, 1790-1860 (Chicago: University of Chicago Press, 1961), 9.

can't be erased. But like the Jews held in slavery in Egypt, God had a plan for their release—starting with "All men are created equal" in the Declaration of Independence to the word "Person" rather than slaves in the body of the Constitution.

The abolition of slavery was slowly picking up steam since the signing of the Declaration of Independence. Between the signing of our independence to the signing of the Constitution, six of the thirteen states had outlawed slavery. In the Constitution, after much debate with the constituents of both sides of the slave argument they wrote in Article IV Section 2 Clause 4 the following:

"No Person held to Service or Labor in one State, under the Laws thereof, escaping into another, shall, in Consequence of any Law or Regulation therein, be discharged from such Service or Labor, but shall be delivered up on Claim of the Party to whom such Service or Labor may be due."

As stated previously, the Founders were very careful with the words they chose to write, and this clause was no different. They are speaking of slaves in the clause, but the wording is very vague. Instead of using the word slave or slavery, they use 'person.' In conjunction with the Declaration of Independence which states, "All men are created equal."

Thomas Jefferson signed the Northwest Ordinance several months before the Constitutional Convention where they discussed and wrote the Constitution. This ordinance gave the land that Virginia owned to the Federal Government to turn into the following states: Ohio, Michigan, Indiana, Illinois, and Wisconsin. A stipulation required by Jefferson before turning the land over was an agreement that slavery would never be allowed in this land. By May of 1790, all thirteen states had ratified the Constitution, and by December of 1865 seventy five years later the thirteenth amendment is ratified to eliminate slavery forever. Today, international slavery is illegal throughout the entire world. Four hundred years of slavery in this country alone ended after seventy years of a document being put in place with nearly nine hundred thousand people dying over a four-year battle; we call the Civil War.

John Adams signed the Declaration of Independence and was the second President of the United States after serving as Vice President for eight years under President George Washington. His son, John Quincy Adams was the sixth President of the United States. He was one of the few Presidents to re-enter politics after serving as President. He became a Congressman and adamantly opposed slavery. His nickname was the "Hell-Hound of Slavery," and he singlehandedly led the fight to lift the 'Gag Rule' which had prohibited discussion of the slavery issue in Congress. He then became a mentor to a freshman Congressman by the name of Abraham Lincoln. John Quincy Adams was asked why he never seemed discouraged or depressed over championing such an unpopular fight against slavery, and he replied: "Duty is ours; results are God's."

The biggest argument of slavery and our Founders today is "why slavery wasn't completely abolished with the writing of the Constitution?" Slavery in the southern states was extremely vital to the economy and their way of life. The delegates from the south would have nothing to do with abolishing slavery. They even threaten to break up the union altogether. The argument over slavery was fierce. Look at Congress today. The Democrats and the Republicans are essentially fierce adversaries. Neither one will break when it comes to compromising on many issues of the day. Our Founders faced the same fierce and maybe worst, situation.

Like a struggling marriage, the husband and wife may be having serious disagreements between each other, but it's important to keep the marriage together while working through the challenges. The Founders temporarily compromised on the slave issue to keep the union together while they worked through the differences.

Over the last 120 years, the progressive movement has controlled the narrative with lies and distortions that today, who would know. Progressives' control academia, the media, both print, and television and much of our political leadership. The truth is still out there, but we must search for it. Meanwhile, progressives are working overtime to erase history which doesn't comply with their narrative. If you question this, ask yourself why you haven't heard about many of the stories mentioned in this book thus far. These stories were common knowledge before the 1900s.

Why is it so important for progressives to remove monuments or distort history? The progressive movement to discredit our Founders is part of the overall strategy to bring Socialism and the New World Order into this country.

The Founders were not perfect—but they had a dream to make this country great, and they accomplished their goal. The baton has been turned over to you and me. Will we tell our grandchildren and their children we dropped the baton, or will they be able to say we ran the good race and won? It's totally up to us, but we must act now.

The Founders on Immigration

The Founders believed immigration was important for the nation and the world. The bases for their stance were on two guiding principles called out in the Declaration of Independence.

1. "We hold these truths to be self-evident, that all men are created equal, that they are endowed by their Creator with certain unalienable rights."
2. "...that among these are Life, Liberty and the pursuit of Happiness.

It's important to note; the Founders always reference back to these two principles and a third which speaks of natural law and natural rights which come from God. Note that America has ALWAYS set limits on immigration. Washington felt immigrants may need to be limited with a view to the qualities of character required for democratic citizenship.

Washington was open to immigration but not unlimited immigration. He believed that immigrants of the wrong sort and in the wrong quantity would endanger American liberty. The purpose of government is to secure the rights to life, liberty, and the pursuit of happiness. Washington stated government requires *"that they who live under its protection should demean themselves as good citizens in giving it on all occasions their effectual support."* He wanted America to become an *"asylum to the virtuous and persecuted part of mankind…"* He also stated to people *"…who are determined to be sober, industrious, and virtuous members of society." "…friends to the rights of mankind." "…a valuable acquisition to our infant settlements."*[137]

As people were migrating to America, they tended to live close to one another in the same area of land. Washington's concern was the immigrants would not assimilate into the fabric of America which was critically important. Washington wrote in a letter to his Vice President John Adams:

> *"The policy or advantage of immigration taking place in a body, (I mean the settling of them in a body) may be much questioned; for, by so doing, they retain the language, habits, and principles (good or bad) which they bring with them. Whereas by an intermixture with our people, they, or their descendants, get assimilated to our customs, measures and laws; in a word, soon become one people."*[138]

Ben Franklin was concerned as well. Franklin felt they wouldn't learn our language and laws which would be detrimental to America. Franklin wrote:

> *"…Yet I am not for refusing entirely to admit them into our colonies; all that seems to be necessary is to distribute them equally, mix them with the English, establish English schools where they are now too thick settled."*[139]

Thomas Jefferson stated his concerns. Like Washington, protecting liberty was his greatest concern. He states:

> *"Every species of government has its specific principles. Ours perhaps are more peculiar than those of any other in the universe. It is a composition of the freest principles of the*

---

137 Washington, G. (n.d.). Founders Online: From George Washington to Francis Adrian Van der Kemp, 28 May … Retrieved February 20, 2018, from https://founders.archives.gov/documents/Washington/04-06-02-0266

138 (15 November 1794, Writings, 34:23, emphasis added. On assimilation, see also Washington to Congress, 8 February 1785, in George Washington: A Collection, 299)

139 Benjamin Franklin to Collinson, 9 May 1753, Writings, ed. J.A. Leo Lemay (New York: Library of America, 1987), 407.

English Constitution, with others derived from natural right and natural reason."[140]

Jefferson is re-iterating our principles which are outlined in the Declaration of Independence. Natural rights and natural reason refer to laws of nature and of Nature's God. Many other Founders had similar concerns. Immigration was important to grow our nation and keep with traditions, but we must never lose sight of the purpose and our privileges as a nation. All immigrants must be willing to assimilate into our country, not change it to the country they came from.

Alexander Hamilton wrote:

"In the recommendation to admit indiscriminately foreign emigrants of every description to the privileges of American citizens, on their first entrance into our country, there is an attempt to break down every pale which has been erected for the reservation of a national spirit and a national character; and to let in the most powerful means of perverting and corrupting both the one and the other."[141]

In Conclusion, immigration is welcome in America. However, not anyone is welcomed. We reserve the right to vet anyone before allowing them to come to America. In no way did the Founders allow just anyone to come in. They must be of a strong moral character and willing to work and contribute to this country. They must be willing to assimilate into our culture and learn our language. They must become Americans.

---

[140] Jefferson, Notes on Virginia (1787), Query 8, Writings, 210-12.
[141] ("The Examination," ns. 7-9 (1802), Papers of Alexander Hamilton, ed. Harold C. Syrett et al. (New York: Columbia University Press, 1961-79),25:491-501)

U.S. Supreme Court in Washington, D.C.

Chapter 8

Original Intent and the Supreme Court

The Founders were careful with the words they chose for the Constitution because power corrupts people and if words could be distorted, they would be. The Founders tried to minimize any misunderstanding of their work—and for a good reason.

Since the progressive era, leaders and organizations have intentionally distorted the historical facts and original intentions for their political agenda. Politically motivated courts have allowed modern-day interpretations of the Founders to influence their decisions—instead of original meanings of the actual words.

When reading the Bible, many of the events and circumstances are unclear without understanding what was happening at the time or what certain phrases mean. For example, in Matthew 19:24, (NIV):

> Jesus says, *"Again I tell you, it is easier for a camel to go through the eye of a needle than for someone who is rich to enter the kingdom of God."*

Taking this scripture at face value, the rich cannot enter the kingdom of heaven. Which raises all kinds of questions like who is considered rich? Is it having a certain dollar amount or the right amount of assets, etc.? If you make $40,000 per year, your income places you at the top 4% of the richest people in the world. In addition, the Bible speaks of many Godly people who are extremely rich. Therefore, it can't be taken at face value or from a modern-day understanding of the words. Plus, the scripture says, "it's easier for a camel" not impossible for a camel to go through an eye of a needle. So, what does: "the eye of the needle" means in Biblical times?

The city gates closed in the evening to keep the enemy from attacking them at night. There was a wall surrounding the city and the only way in after the gates closed was through a small door. When a citizen approached the small door with his camel, he would unload everything from the camel's back. The camel would drop to its knees and crawl through the small opening. The owner would walk everything through the entrance and re-load it back on the camel and continue home. This opening was called the "eye of the needle."

The "eye of the needle" 2000 years ago means something totally different than it does today. The same is true 250 years ago and why it's important for us to research and understand the original intent of the writings. This isn't new to the courts. They understand what original intent means but are ruling based on political expediency. This is "bad behavior," and the judges should be removed from the bench. It's why we have distorted decision which is exemplified in our court systems today.

In David Barton's book, 'Original Intent' (Barton, 1996, 2000, 2008, 2011) he poses several questions and then proceeds to thoroughly answer each one. Here are two distinct points I want to quote:

- "Since Jefferson has over sixty volumes of written works and Madison has over twenty, why does the Court continually invoke only one or two select sentences from these exhaustive works? Is it perhaps that the rest of the statements made by Madison and Jefferson reveal the Court's intentional miss-portrayal of their intent?"[142]
- "Since several signers of the Constitution were also Justices on the U.S. Supreme Court, why does the current Court avoid citing the declarations of those Justices on today's issues? Is it perhaps that the concise rulings of those who so clearly understood constitutional intent would contradict and thus embarrass the Court for its current positions?"[143]

---

[142] Barton, D. (2011). *Original Intent: The Courts, the Constitution, and Religion* (5th ed.). Aledo, TX: WallBuilder Press. p.6

[143] Barton, D. (2011). *Original Intent: The Courts, the Constitution, and Religion* (5th ed.). Aledo, TX: WallBuilder Press.

Barton also points out that "there were fifty-five Founders who drafted the Constitution and an additional ninety more who drafted the Bill of Rights." So why do the modern-day courts only use quotes from Jefferson and Madison? Is it because they could only find so many quotes that could be distorted to accommodate their political agenda?

Here are several quotes from our Founders regarding the importance of using the original intent when making decisions.

In an exchange with then-President Thomas Jefferson and Supreme Court Justice William Johnson, Jefferson states:

> *"On every question of construction, carry ourselves back to the time when the Constitution was adopted, recollect the spirit manifested in the debates, and instead of trying what meaning may be squeezed out of the text, or invented against it, conform to the probable one is which it was passed"*[144]

Or James Madison who said:

> *"I entirely concur in the propriety of resorting to the sense in which the Constitution was accepted and ratified by the nation. In that sense alone, it is the legitimate Constitution. And if that be not the guide in expounding it, there can be no security for a consistent and stable, more than for a faithful, exercise of its powers...What a metamorphosis would be produced in the code of law if all its ancient phraseology were to be taken in its modern sense."*[145]

Madison clearly states that even back then; they must have the proper understanding of the language to know what the actual intent of the original writings was.

Today, when we look at our appointed justices, we must choose a judge that is an "originalist." One who rules on the

---

[144] Thomas Jefferson, Memoir, Correspondence, and Miscellanies, From the Papers of Thomas Jefferson, Thomas Jefferson Randolph, editor (Boston: Gray and Bowen, 1830), Vol. IV, p.373, to Judge William Johnson, June 12, 1823.

[145] James Madison, The Writings of James Madison, Gaillard Hunt, editor (New York: G.P. Putnam's Sons, 1910), Vol. IX, p.191, to Henry Lee, June 25, 1824

original intent of the Founders and doesn't deliver decisions based on political partisanship.

United States Supreme Court

Chapter 4 discussed our Founder's faith in God. We learned Christianity was a critical part of our republican form of government. When a republican style government doesn't follow Judeo-Christian principles, it won't survive.

This chapter will look at many of the early Supreme Court cases and see the beliefs of our Founders was prevalent in the decisions of the courts as well. A review of these early decisions will prove that progressivism has infiltrated the court systems of today.

1844, in the case of Vidal vs. Girard's Executors, 43 U.S. 126, 132, Justice Joseph Story delivered the court's opinion. The case concerned one Stephen Girard, a deist from France, who had moved to Philadelphia and later died. In his will he left his entire estate, valued at over $7 million, to establish an orphanage and school, with the stipulation that no religious influence be allowed. The city rejected the proposal, as their lawyers declared:[146]

> The plan of education proposed is anti-Christian, and therefore repugnant to the law... The purest principles of morality are to be taught. Where are they found? Whoever searches for them must go to the source from which a Christian man derives his faith—the Bible...There is an obligation to teach what the Bible alone can teach, viz. a pure system of morality...
>
> Both in the Old and New Testaments importance is recognized. In the Old it is said, "thou shalt diligently teach them to thy children," and the New, "Suffer the little children to come unto me and forbid them not..." No fault can be found with Girard for wishing a marble college to

---

[146] Federer, W. J. (1994). America's God and Country. Coppell, Texas: Fame Publishing, Inc. p. 595

bear his name forever, but it is not valuable unless it has a fragrance of Christianity about it.[147]

The U.S. Supreme Court rendered its unanimous opinion, stating: Christianity...is not to be maliciously and openly reviled and blasphemed against, to the annoyance of deliverers or the injury of the public...It is unnecessary for us, however, to consider the establishment of a school or college, for the propagation of ...Deism, or any other form of infidelity. Such a case is not to be presumed to exist in a Christian country...why may not laymen instruct in the general principles of Christianity as well as ecclesiastics... And we cannot overlook the blessing, which such laymen by their conduct, as well as their instructions, may, nay must impart to their youthful pupils. Why may not the Bible, and especially the New Testament, without note or comment, be read and taught as a divine revelation in the school—its general precepts expounded, its evidence explained, and its glorious principles of morality inculcated?... Where can the purest principles of morality be learned so clearly or so perfectly as from the New Testament?[148] It is also said, and truly that the Christian religion is a part of the common law of Pennsylvania...[149]

In 1878, the Supreme Court rendered its opinion on the case of Reynolds vs. United States, 98 U.S 145, 165. The court ruled in favor of very strict laws against polygamy and sexual immorality. This decision was based on religious freedom.

In 1885 The Supreme Court ruled in the case of Murphy vs. Ramsey and Others, 144 U.S. 15, 45 gave its opinion: The Court

---

[147] United States Supreme Court. 1844, Vidal v. Girard's Executors, 43 U.S. 126, 132, 143, 152-153, 170, 175, (1844). David Barton, The Myth of Separation (Aledo, TX: WallBuilder Press, 1991), pp. 61-62
[148] United States Supreme Court. 1844, Vidal v. Girard's Executors, 43 U.S. 126, 132, (1844), pp. 198, 205-206. David Barton, The Myth of Separation (Aledo, TX: WallBuilder Press, 1991), pp. 62-63
[149] United States Supreme Court.1892, Justice Brewer, Church of the Holy Trinity v. United States, 143 US 457,458, 465-471,36L ed 226. David Barton, The Myth of Separation (Aledo, TX: WallBuilder Press, 1991), pp. 47-51

ruled in favor of a marriage of "the union for life of one man and one woman in the holy estate of matrimony."

In 1889, the case of Davis vs. Beason, 133 U. S. 333,341-343. Samuel Davis was caught in the crime of bigamy and polygamy. His case went to the Supreme Court because he believed it was his religious belief that he should have the freedom to commit bigamy and polygamy under the First Amendment.

> The Supreme Court ruled: Bigamy and polygamy are crimes by the laws of all civilized and Christian countries. ...They destroy the purity of the marriage relation, to disturb the peace of families, to degrade woman and debase man...To call their advocacy a tenet of religion is to offend the commons sense of mankind...[150]

The next Supreme Court ruling below expresses America's Christian heritage as important to the decision process made in this ruling. Not all the Christian references were included here— but enough to make the point.

On February 29, 1892, in the case of Church of the Holy Trinity vs. United States, 143 U.S. 457-458, 465-471, 36 L ed. 226 the Court ruled:

> Our laws and our institutions must necessarily be based upon and embody the teachings of the Redeemer of mankind (Jesus Christ). It is impossible that it should be otherwise; and in this sense and to this extent our civilization and our institutions are emphatically Christian...The commission to Christopher Columbus...(recited) that it is hoped that by God's assistance some of the continents and islands in the ocean will be discovered...The celebrated compact made by the Pilgrims in the Mayflower, 1620, recites: "Having undertaken for the Glory of God, and advancement of the Christian faith...And well knowing where a people are

---

[150] United States Supreme Court. 1889, Davis v. Beason, 133 U.S. 333,341-343, 348 (1890). David Barton, The Myth of Separation (Aledo, TX: WallBuilder Press, 1991), pp. 67-69

gathered together the word of God requires that to maintain the peace and union...there should be an orderly and decent government established according to God...to maintain and preserve the liberty and purity of the gospel of our Lord Jesus which we now profess...

Coming nearer to the present time, the Declaration of Independence recognizes the presence of the Divine in human affairs in these words: (the Judge than quotes the Declaration of Independence).

(The Judge continues): ...We find everywhere a clear recognition of the same truth...because of a general recognition of this truth that we are a Christian nation, the question has seldom been presented to the courts...These are not individual sayings, declarations of private persons: they are organic utterances; they speak the voice of the entire people.

This Judge then quotes several other rulings, not covered here, but to continue with the key points.

...The Commonwealth, it was decided that, Christianity, general Christianity, is, and always has been, a part of the common law...not Christianity with an established church...but Christianity with liberty of conscience to all men.

The Judge continues quoting even another case:

...The people of this State, in common with the people of this country, profess the general doctrines of Christianity, as the rule of their faith and practice...We are a Christian people, and the morality of the country is deeply engrafted upon Christianity, and not upon the doctrines or worship of those impostors (other religions)... "It is also said, and truly, that the Christian religion is a part of the common law..."

This Judge continues with many more examples, but I'll end with this:

> These, and many other matters which might be noticed, add a volume of unofficial declarations to the mass of organic utterances that this is a Christian nation...we find everywhere a clear recognition of the same truth.
> The happiness of a people and the good order and preservation of civil government essentially depend upon piety, religion and morality.[151]
> Religion, morality, and knowledge are necessary to good government, the preservation of liberty, and the happiness of mankind.[152]

> In a case, 1931, United States vs Macintosh, 283 U.S. 605, 625: The Court ruling was as follows: We are a Christian people...according to one another the equal right of religious freedom and acknowledge with reverence the duty of obedience to the will of God.[153]
> In a case, 1948, McCollum vs Board of Education, 333 U.S. 203 court's opinion:

> Traditionally, organized education in the Western world was Church education. It could hardly be otherwise when the education of children was primarily study of the Word and the ways of God. Even in the Protestant countries, where there was a less close identification of Church and State, the basis of education was largely the Bible, and its chief purpose inculcation of piety...[154]

The Supreme Court cases thus far have made the case that the United States of America is a Christian nation. That Jesus

---

[151] United States Supreme Court. 1892, Church of the Holy Trinity v. U.S., 143 U.S. 457,469 (1892). David Barton, The Myth of Separation (Aledo, TX: WallBuilder Press, 1991), p. 247

[152] United States Supreme Court. 1892, Church of the Holy Trinity v. U.S., 143 U.S. 457,469 (1892). David Barton, The Myth of Separation (Aledo, TX: WallBuilder Press, 1991), p. 248

[153] United States Supreme Court. 1931, Justice George Sutherland, (reviewing the 1892 decision), United States v. Macintosh, 283 U.S. 605, 625 1931, David Barton, The Myth of Separation (Aledo, TX: WallBuilder Press, 1991), p. 76

[154] United States Supreme Court. 1948, Justice Frankfurter, McCollum v. Board of Education, 333 U.S. 203. John Eidsmoe, God & Caesar—Christian Faith & Political Action (Westchester, IL: Crossway Books, a Division of Good News Publishers, 1984), pp. 140-141.

Christ is at the center of all decision made. The Bible was critical to the moral fiber of the nation. There were many other cases which could've been presented here. However, these are some of the stronger cases to make the point.

Next, are also cases that stand up for God and Christianity but notice the wording has become watered down a bit. The points made are not as strong as they were in previous years. These Supreme Court rulings fall 40 plus years after the progressive movement began. At this point, Progressivism had begun to influence many of our political leaders, justices, educators, and media.

Bullet point marks are used to mark the keywords made in the court decision to keep the chapter short:

In the case, 1952, of Zorach vs. Clauson, 343 U.S. 306 307 313, the decision stated:

- The First Amendment, however, does not say that in every respect there shall be a separation of Church and State...
- ...Otherwise the state and religion would be aliens to each other—hostile, suspicious, and even unfriendly...
- Municipalities would not be permitted to render police or fire protection to religious groups. Policemen who helped parishioners into their places of worship would violate the Constitution. Prayers in our legislative halls; the appeals to the Almighty in the messages of the Chief Executive; the proclamation making Thanksgiving Day a holiday; "so help me God" in our courtroom oaths—these and all other references to the Almighty that run through our laws, our public rituals, our ceremonies, would be flouting the First Amendment. A fastidious atheist or agnostic could even object to the supplication with which the Court opens each session: God save the United States and this Honorable Court.
- We are a religious people, and our institutions presuppose a Supreme Being...
- ...That would be preferring those who believe in no religion over those who do believe...

- We cannot read into the Bill of Rights such a philosophy of hostility to religion.[155]

In the case, 1963, School District of Abington Township vs. Schempp, 374 U.S. 203, 212, 225

- It is true that religion has been closely identified with our history and government...The history of man is inseparable from the history of religion.
- Secularism is unconstitutional...preferring those who do not believe over those who do believe...
- It is the duty of government to deter no-belief religions...
- Facilities of government cannot offend religious principles...
- The State may not establish a 'religion of secularism' in the sense of affirmatively opposing or showing hostility to religion, thus preferring those who believe in no religion over those who do believe.
- ...It certainly may be said that the Bible is worthy of study for its literary and historic qualities. Nothing we have said here indicates that such study of the Bible or of religion, when presented objectively as part of a secular program of education, may not be affected consistently with the First Amendment.[156]

In the case, 1980, Stone vs Graham, 449 U.S. 39, 42, 46 stated:

- ...The Bible may constitutionally be used in an appropriate study of history, civilization, ethics, comparative religion, or the like.[157]

---

[155] United States Supreme Court. 1952, Justice William O. Douglas, Zorach v. Clauson, 343 US 306 307 312-315 (1952). Dr. Ed Rowe, The ACLU and America's Freedom (Washington: Church League of America, 1984), pp. 20-21

[156] United States Supreme Court. 1963, Abington Township v. Schempp, 374 U.S. 203, 225, 300-301 (1963), Associate Justice Tom Clark writing the Court's opinion, Justice William Joseph Brennan, Jr. concurring. Jay Sekulow, Letter to School Superintendents (Virginia Beach, VA: American Center for Law and Justice, November 17, 1992), p. 1.

[157] United States Supreme Court. 1980, Stone v. Graham, 449 U.S. 39, 42 (1980). Jay Sekulow, Letter to School Superintendents (Virginia Beach, VA: American Center for Law and Justice, November 17, 1992), p. 1.

In the case, 1982, Chambers vs. Marsh, 675 F. 2d 228, 233, the decision stated:

- ...The men who wrote the First Amendment religion clause did not view paid legislative chaplains and opening prayers as a violation of that amendment...the practice of opening sessions with prayer has continued without interruption ever since that early session of Congress.[158]
- It can hardly be thought that in the same week the members of the first Congress voted to appoint and pay a chaplain for each House and voted to approve the draft of the First Amendment...that they intended to forbid what they had just declared acceptable.[159]
- Chaplains and prayers are deeply embedded in the history and tradition of this country.[160]

In the case, 1985, of Lynch vs. Donnelly 465 U.S.668,669-670, the case was brought up against the city of Pawtucket, R.I. who were putting up a nativity display and had been for 200 years. The decision came down as:

- The creche (nativity) display is sponsored by the city to celebrate the Holiday recognized by Congress and national tradition and to depict the origins of that Holiday; these are legitimate secular purposes...The creche is no more an advancement or endorsement of religion than the congressional and executive recognition of the origins of Christmas...[161]

---

[158] United States Supreme Court. 1982, Chambers v. Marsh, 675 F. 2d 228, 233 (8th Cir. 1982); review allowed, 463 U.S. 783 (1982), Chief Justice Warren Earl Burger. "Our Christian Heritage," Letter from Plymouth Rock (Marlborough, NH: The Plymouth Rock Foundation), p. 7.

[159] United States Supreme Court. 1982, Chambers v. Marsh, 675 F. 2d 228, 233 (8th Cir. 1982); review allowed, 463 U.S. 783 (1982), Chief Justice Warren Earl Burger. Tracy Everbach, Dallas Morning News, March 16, 1993, pp. 1A, 8A.

[160] United States Supreme Court. 1982, Chambers v. Marsh, 675 F. 2d 228, 233 (8th Cir. 1982); review allowed, 463 U.S. 783 (1982), Chief Justice Warren Earl Burger. Tracy Everbach, Dallas Morning News, March 16, 1993, pp. 1A, 8A.

[161] United States Supreme Court. 1985, Lynch v. Donnelly, 465 U.S. 668, 669-670, 673 (1985), Chief Justice Warren Burger. David Barton, The Myth of Separation (Aledo, TX: WallBuilder Press, 1991), p. 189

- There is an unbroken history of official acknowledgment by all three branches of government of the role of religion in American life...
- The Constitution does not require a complete separation of church and state. It affirmatively mandates accommodation, not merely tolerance, of all religions and forbids hostility towards any.[162]

In the case, 1985, Wallace vs. Jafree, 472 U.S.,38,99 the decision stated:

- ...The establishment clause had been expressly freighted with Jefferson's misleading metaphor for nearly forty years...
- There is simply no historical foundation for the proposition that the framers intended to build a wall of separation between church and state... The recent court decisions are in no way based on either the language or intent of the framers.[163]

The Federalist and Anti-Federalist Papers

The theme throughout this book is the Founders were passionate men that wanted "life, liberty and happiness" for the citizens of America. They were striving to design the best form of government possible for the American people. It wasn't about money, power or fame—just a passion for America to be great. Looking at the Federalist Papers and compare them to the Anti-Federalist Papers, it's like two sides of the same coin. When the coin was tossed, Heads won (The Federalist Papers). This in no way meant that the tails (The Anti-Federalist Papers) were any less of value. It's the same coin. The men of both sides of the coin had America's best interest in mind.

The Federalist papers were written as a commentary to the Constitution. They discuss each point of the Constitution and why it was written as is. The Anti-Federalist felt that the

---

[162] United States Supreme Court. 1985, Lynch v. Donnelly, 465 U.S. 668, 669-670, 673 (1985), Chief Justice Warren Burger. David Barton, The Myth of Separation (Aledo, TX: WallBuilder Press, 1991), p. 189

[163] United States Supreme Court. 1985, Wallace v. Jafree, 472 U.S., 38, 99. "Our Christian Heritage," Letter from Plymouth Rock (Marlborough, NH: The Plymouth rock Foundation), p. 8.

Constitution didn't go far enough in limiting the powers of the Federal Government. They weren't against the Constitution; they just felt it wasn't complete—it needed a Bill of Rights.

Two hundred and thirty years later we can look at the Anti-Federalist Papers and see they were right in many cases. The Constitution wasn't wrong—it just could have gone further in some of its limitations.

Why were the Federalist Papers written? Article 5 of the Constitution requires that three-quarters of all states must ratify the amendment for it to become a part of the Constitution. The same was required of the original Constitution before it became the law of the land. There was plenty of opposition to ratifying the Constitution in New York (Anti-Federalist). The current Governor George Clinton was one of the major decenters.

James Madison, Alexander Hamilton and John Jay decided to write essays for three of the New York newspapers. They discussed each aspect of the Constitution and why it's important for New York to ratify it. Also, Hamilton and Jay were from New York and wanted their state to have ratified the document. The three Founders wrote their essays using the pen name of Publius. Publius Valerius Publicola was a man that established the republican form of government in Ancient Rome. The first of these papers, known as the opening remarks was written and published by Alexander Hamilton on October 27, 1787. The final paper, number eighty-five or the conclusion, was also written by Hamilton and it was published August 13, 1788.

Delaware started the ratifying convention process on December 4, 1787, and by December 7th had ratified the Constitution at which point sixteen of the eighty-five papers had been printed. Pennsylvania was second to ratify on December 12, 1787. Next was New Jersey on December 18, 1787, followed by Georgia on December 31, Connecticut on January 9, 1788, Massachusetts on February 6th, Maryland on April 26th, and South Carolina on the 23rd of May. By this point, seventy-seventh papers had been written. Eight states had ratified the Constitution, and only one more state was needed. On June 21, 1788, New Hampshire became the ninth and final state that was needed to make the Constitution the law of the land. Virginia rolled in next as the tenth on June 25th, and New York was the eleventh on July

26, 1788. By the closing of the New York convention the eighty-fourth paper had been published. On November 21, 1789, came North Carolina and finally on May 29, 1790, came Rhode Island to make it unanimous. All thirteen states had successfully ratified the Constitution of the United States of America.

Did the Federalist Papers have an impact on the ratifying of the Constitution? You could argue very little if any since the papers were originally written in New York newspapers alone and ten of the nine states, needed to ratify the Constitution were already in. Nor is it likely the people in the other states read the papers via email or internet at that time. Although it's possible, they received the papers days or even weeks later.

Then why are the Federalist papers so well thought of? Thomas Jefferson is quoted as saying the Federalist Papers are "the best commentary on the principles of government, which ever was written." The Supreme Court has used the Federalist papers in making decisions based on the original intent of the Founders. Today, if you want to understand the Founders perspective of the Constitution you should read and study the Federalist Papers.

As stated, not all the Founders were thrilled with this Constitution. Many felt it must have a Bill of Rights to protect the liberty of the people. They were concerned the federal government would be too powerful, and the states would lose the power designated to them. Others weren't happy with the way the judicial system was set up. Some didn't like having a President overseeing everything. The Founders were concerned this new President would eventually turn into a Monarchy. Like Hamilton, Madison and Jay these Founders also expressed their concerns by writing articles in the newspapers. These papers are called the Anti-Federalist papers, and the men who wrote them used pen names of Brutus and Cato.

Hamilton wrote in Federalist paper number eighty-four why a Bill of Rights wasn't necessary. However, with the opposition from the Anti-Federalist and the compromise made with North Carolina and Rhode Island—a Bill of Rights was written and ratified by December 15, 1791.

Interesting notes about the Federalist Papers: They were eighty-five well written and organized papers. The structure of all the Federalist Papers was to coincide with the Constitution itself.

They were written and organized by just three people who felt the Constitution was the answer to the challenges the country was having with a weak federal government.

On the other hand, the Anti-Federalist Papers were written randomly by many different men with no real structure. It appears each letter was written base on what the author felt was the next best argument to make. It wasn't till the twentieth century that the papers were even combined to one sort of book. Gratefully their argument was heard because without the Bill of Rights we may have bigger challenges as a country today than we do now. Some of the notable authors of the Anti-Federalist papers were: Patrick Henry, Samuel Adams, George Mason, James Monroe, John DeWitt, Richard Henry Lee, George Clinton, and about half a dozen other men.

The British surrender at Yorktown. General Benjamin Lincoln (white horse in the middle). George Washington with the American officers on the right and the French officers on the left.

Chapter 9

Understanding the Declaration of Independence

In the following chapters, we'll analyze both the Declaration of Independence and the Constitution of the United States. Afterward, you'll have a working knowledge of these founding documents in a fundamental, reader's digest kind of way. We will:

- Reference back to topics we learned earlier pointing out significant factors
- Understand how the two documents relate to one another
- Touch on areas that have been subverted by our government
- Learn why we need to get back to the "original intent" of these documents.

These God-inspired documents have set the foundation for an amazing country you and I call The United States of America.

Now, there were numerous events and circumstances that led to the significance of the Declaration of Independence, but I want to cover just two of them before breaking down the document: the Boston Tea Party and a pamphlet called Common Sense written by Thomas Paine.

The Boston Tea Party

Due to Great Britain's financial woes from their war with France, England needed to raise money to help pay for the war, so they passed several new Acts charging the American colonies taxes on goods that were shipped to America. One of these Acts was the Tea Act in the summer of 1773. The Tea Act was designed to help a political ally to the King by essentially granting a monopoly to the East India Company and taxing the colonies for this tea. Several of the states refused the tea and sent the ships back to England. The Royal Governor of Massachusetts decided to keep the tea and allow the tea to be unloaded from the ships. On December 16, 1773, a group of men led by Samuel Adams dressed up as Indians, boarded the ships in the middle of the night and dumped the tea into the Boston Harbor. Hence the famous name, the Boston tea party. This and other acts of protest from the thirteen colonies resulted in escalating tension between Great Britain and the United States ultimately leading to the Revolutionary War.

Common Sense by Thomas Paine

On January 10, 1776, almost six months before the signing of the Declaration of Independence Thomas Paine wrote a pamphlet called "Common Sense." The pamphlet described the difference between a monarchical form of government as opposed to a republican form of government. He discusses biblically how God did not want the people of Israel to have a king, but the people of Israel wanted a king because all the other countries had a king. He argued against popular thought used to justify a king—and referenced the Bible and their history with England. Thomas Paine's argument relates so well to what's happening in America today. We don't have a king per se, but the progressives in Washington D.C. have acquired too much power over the last hundred plus years which resemble having a king. Paine's writings inspired people in the 13 states which prepared their hearts to fight the greatest military in the world for an opportunity at achieving total freedom. To this day, his writings are still being published.

The Declaration of Independence

Note: the BOLD print is the actual wording of the original documents, and the regular print is the commentary on the sentence or paragraph. The spelling is from the original document.

IN CONGRESS, July 4, 1776.
The unanimous Declaration of the thirteen United States of America,

Thomas Jefferson is credited with writing this document in a committee with Ben Franklin, John Adams, Roger Sherman, and Robert Livingston. They wrote it in 17 days and submitted it to Congress on June 28, 1776. It was voted on and rejected on July 2, 1776. The Founders edited it and then adopted it with a unanimous vote on July 4th, 1776.

When in the Course of human events, it becomes necessary for one people to dissolve the political bands which have connected them with another, and to assume among the powers of the earth, the separate and equal station to which the Laws of Nature and of Nature's God entitle them, a decent respect to the opinions of mankind requires that they should declare the causes which impel them to the separation.

The Founding Fathers get straight to the point in the first paragraph. They declared to the King of England they wanted a separation from Great Britain. The political ties between to two countries were to be dissolved.

The first of four references to God are written here as well. They claim *"the Laws of Nature and of Nature's God"* entitle them to be a separate and equal nation no longer under England's authority.

We hold these truths to be self-evident, that all men are created equal, that they are endowed by their Creator with certain unalienable Rights, that among these are Life, Liberty and the pursuit of Happiness.,

These are the most recognized and spoken words of either this document or the Constitution. You may recall these are several of the lines Woodrow Wilson wanted you to ignore because they're detrimental to the progressive movement.

These powerful words say so much— *"We hold these truths to be self-evident."* Jefferson states the following truths cannot be disputed, especially in reference to God.

The dictionary definition of truth is *Conformity to fact or reality; exact accordance with that which is or has been or shall be.*[164]

Self-evident means: *Evident without proof or reasoning; that produces certainty or clear conviction upon a bare presentation to the mind.*[165]

Therefore, the following facts do not need to be demonstrated or explained. They are absolute truths. Now for the truths, *"all men are created equal."* Jefferson states ALL men, regardless of race or gender. This document is God inspired, and therefore all men are created equal whether man, woman, black or white.

Endowed means: *furnished with a portion of estate; supplied with a permanent fund.*

To paraphrase: The God of the Universe has given us certain rights that are impossible to take away by any man or government. Since these rights are given to us by God and not the government, the government has no authority to take them away.

This explains why the elitists in our government want to remove God from the public square. If God is irrelevant in the matters of government, then it can be assumed our rights come from government and not from God. Therefore, they can also be taken away. In addition, if we don't understand our rights, then we won't know when these rights have been violated.

"that among these are Life, Liberty and the pursuit of Happiness.,

Life: no one has the right to take our life. We have every right to live as anyone else.

Liberty: consists in the power of acting as one thinks fit, without any restraint or control, except from the laws of nature.[166]

---

164 Webster, N. (1995). An American dictionary of the English language: an introductory dissertation of the origin, history and connection of the language of Western Asia, and of Europe and a concise grammar of the English language. San Francisco, CA: The Foundation for American Christian Education.
165 Webster, N. (1995). An American dictionary of the English language: an introductory dissertation of the origin, history and connection of the language of Western Asia, and of Europe and a concise grammar of the English language. San Francisco, CA: The Foundation for American Christian Education.
166 Webster, N. (1995). An American dictionary of the English language: an introductory dissertation of the origin, history and connection of the language of Western Asia, and of Europe and a concise grammar of the English language. San Francisco, CA: The Foundation for American Christian Education.

The pursuit of happiness: there are several views as to this meaning. I recommend you research to find out for yourself, but the best definition I could find is—to pursue things that can make a positive difference in our families lives and the lives of our fellow Americans. By doing this, we will experience our own sense of happiness. This can mean utilizing the free enterprise system to make or build a business, or pursuing the virtues of life and helping to bestow them on others, i.e., sharing your Christian faith, etc.

That to secure these rights, Governments are instituted among Men, deriving their just powers from the consent of the governed,

Jefferson is saying we have God-given rights that must be protected. We've granted limited powers to the government to protect our rights. Since the British government neglected and refused to protect our rights, we will establish a new government which will receive its power from the consent of the people. These powers include protecting our country from both foreign and domestic threats.

That whenever any Form of Government becomes destructive of these ends, it is the Right of the People to alter or to abolish it, and to institute new Government, laying its foundation on such principles and organizing its powers in such form, as to them shall seem most likely to affect their Safety and Happiness.

Great Britain was acting in a tyrannical fashion, and it was time to put an end to the political relationship between the two countries. Today our government has usurped many of our freedoms and is working hard to remove more of our rights each day. Article V of the Constitution of the United States gives "We the People" a modern-day way of fixing our government. We will discuss this in chapter 18. Also note, *"...it is the Right of the People to alter or to abolish it, and to institute new Government,"* This is a safeguard for today as well. The Founders gave us the second amendment as a safeguard to help prevent our government from becoming a totalitarian country.

Prudence, indeed, will dictate that Governments long established should not be changed for light and transient causes; and accordingly all experience hath shewn, that mankind are more disposed to suffer, while evils are

sufferable, than to right themselves by abolishing the forms to which they are accustomed. But when a long train of abuses and usurpations, pursuing invariably the same Object evinces a design to reduce them under absolute Despotism, it is their right, it is their duty, to throw off such Government, and to provide new Guards for their future security

Jefferson states, we understand—to throw out a government for minor and relatively inconsequential infractions could create more problems than maintaining the status quo and trying to work them out. He states, however, *"but when a long train of abuses and usurpations..."* are taking place and there doesn't seem to be an alternative solution then we must move forward with a new form of government.

Despotism means: *Absolute power; authority unlimited and uncontrolled by men, constitution or laws and depending alone on the will of the prince.*[167]

When you read the twenty-seven grievances that are outlined below, you will see some of the cruel and unfair ways of how the King did rule.

Such has been the patient sufferance of these Colonies; and such is now the necessity which constrains them to alter their former Systems of Government. The history of the present King of Great Britain is a history of repeated injuries and usurpations, all having in direct object the establishment of an absolute Tyranny over these States. To prove this, let Facts be submitted to a candid world

This is the opening argument against the king. The king assumed power over the colonies both illegally and by force and exercised this power in cruel and arbitrary ways over a long period of time.

The following is a list of all the infractions that the colonies have against the king. Many of which are called out in the United States Constitution as answers to protecting the people, so the new government does not create the same infractions.

Assent means: *to admit as true; to agree, yield or concede, or rather to express an agreement of the mind to what is alleged or proposed.*

---

[167] Webster, N. (1995). An American dictionary of the English language: an introductory dissertation of the origin, history and connection of the language of Western Asia, and of Europe and a concise grammar of the English language. San Francisco, CA: The Foundation for American Christian Education.

Redress means: *to set right; to amend.*
1.He has refused his Assent to Laws, the most wholesome and necessary for the public good.
2. He has forbidden his Governors to pass Laws of immediate and pressing importance, unless suspended in their operation till his Assent should be obtained; and when so suspended, he has utterly neglected to attend to them.
3. He has refused to pass other Laws for the accommodation of large districts of people, unless those people would relinquish the right of Representation in the Legislature, a right inestimable to them and formidable to tyrants only.
4. He has called together legislative bodies at places unusual, uncomfortable, and distant from the depository of their public Records, for the sole purpose of fatiguing them into compliance with his measures.
5. He has dissolved Representative Houses repeatedly, for opposing with manly firmness his invasions on the rights of the people.
6. He has refused for a long time, after such dissolutions, to cause others to be elected; whereby the Legislative powers, incapable of Annihilation, have returned to the People at large for their exercise; the State remaining in the meantime exposed to all the dangers of invasion from without, and convulsions within.
7. He has endeavored to prevent the population of these States; for that purpose obstructing the Laws for Naturalization of Foreigners; refusing to pass others to encourage their migrations hither, and raising the conditions of new Appropriations of Lands.
8. He has obstructed the Administration of Justice, by refusing his Assent to Laws for establishing Judiciary powers.
9. He has made Judges dependent on his Will alone, for the tenure of their offices, and the amount and payment of their salaries.
10. He has erected a multitude of New Offices, and sent hither swarms of Officers to harass our people, and eat out their substance.
11. He has kept among us, in times of peace, Standing Armies without the Consent of our legislatures.

12. He has affected to render the Military independent of and superior to the Civil power.

13. He has combined with others to subject us to a jurisdiction foreign to our constitution, and unacknowledged by our laws; giving his Assent to their Acts of pretended Legislation:

14. For Quartering large bodies of armed troops among us:

15. For protecting them, by a mock Trial, from punishment for any Murders which they should commit on the Inhabitants of these States:

16. For cutting off our Trade with all parts of the world:

17. For imposing Taxes on us without our Consent:

18. For depriving us in many cases, of the benefits of Trial by Jury:

19. For transporting us beyond Seas to be tried for pretended offences

20. For abolishing the free System of English Laws in a neighboring Province, establishing therein an Arbitrary government, and enlarging its Boundaries so as to render it at once an example and fit instrument for introducing the same absolute rule into these Colonies:

21. For taking away our Charters, abolishing our most valuable Laws, and altering fundamentally the Forms of our Governments:

22. For suspending our own Legislatures and declaring themselves invested with power to legislate for us in all cases whatsoever.

23. He has abdicated Government here, by declaring us out of his Protection and waging War against us.

24. He has plundered our seas, ravaged our Coasts, burnt our towns, and destroyed the lives of our people.

25. He is at this time transporting large Armies of foreign Mercenaries to complete the works of death, desolation and tyranny, already begun with circumstances of Cruelty & perfidy scarcely paralleled in the most barbarous ages, and totally unworthy the Head of a civilized nation.

26. He has constrained our fellow Citizens taken Captive on the high Seas to bear Arms against their Country, to become the executioners of their friends and Brethren, or to fall themselves by their Hands.

27. He has excited domestic insurrections amongst us, and has endeavored to bring on the inhabitants of our frontiers, the merciless Indian Savages, whose known rule of warfare, is an undistinguished destruction of all ages, sexes and conditions.

Note, the original text of the Declaration of Independence does not number the grievances against the king. They're numbered here to be referenced later in the book as they relate to the Constitution of the United States. There are 27 grievances outlined against King George. Many of these grievances made it difficult to run a nation efficiently while other grievances are cruel and unusual powers against the people of the United States.

In every stage of these Oppressions We have petitioned for Redress in the most humble terms: Our repeated Petitions have been answered only by repeated injury. A Prince, whose character is thus marked by every act which may define a Tyrant, is unfit to be the ruler of a free people.

Nor have We been wanting in attentions to our British brethren. We have warned them from time to time of attempts by their legislature to extend an unwarrantable jurisdiction over us. We have reminded them of the circumstances of our emigration and settlement here. We have appealed to their native justice and magnanimity, and we have conjured them by the ties of our common kindred to disavow these usurpations, which would inevitably interrupt our connections and correspondence. They too have been deaf to the voice of justice and of consanguinity. We must, therefore, acquiesce in the necessity, which denounces our Separation, and hold them, as we hold the rest of mankind, Enemies in War, in Peace Friends.

The colonies tried to have a dialog with the King over these grievances—but he just doubled down on his oppression. They even reached out to the people of England and the King's justices but to no avail. All fell on deaf ears, and nothing had come of their efforts. The Founders felt they had no other recourse but to dissolve the political relationship between America and Great Britain.

We, therefore, the Representatives of the United States of America, in General Congress, Assembled, appealing to the

Supreme Judge of the world for the rectitude of our intentions, do, in the Name, and by Authority of the good People of these Colonies, solemnly publish and declare, That these United Colonies are, and of Right ought to be Free and Independent States; that they are Absolved from all Allegiance to the British Crown, and that all political connection between them and the State of Great Britain, is and ought to be totally dissolved; and that as Free and Independent States, they have full Power to levy War, conclude Peace, contract Alliances, establish Commerce, and to do all other Acts and Things which Independent States may of right do. And for the support of this Declaration, with a firm reliance on the protection of divine Providence, we mutually pledge to each other our Lives, our Fortunes and our sacred Honor.

Jefferson makes his closing statement to the King of England and the rest of the world. Note, the third and fourth reference to God is clearly stated. They are *"appealing to the Supreme Judge of the world"* (God) and *"with a firm reliance on the protection of divine Providence"* (God). Each person that signed the Declaration of Independence knew they just signed their death warrant. John Hancock said in Congress, *"having signed the Declaration, must now all hang together"* and Benjamin Franklin replied: *"Yes, we must indeed all hang together, or most assuredly we shall all hang separately."* Finally, they end it with: *"we mutually pledge to each other our Lives, our Fortunes and our sacred Honor."* Are modern-day Americans ready to pledge our lives, fortunes, and sacred honor to take back our nation? Are we willing to seek the truth? Are we willing to learn and study the Constitution of the United States and know it like the back of our hand? By doing so, we can hold our politicians accountable, and this American experiment will survive.

Chapter 10

Understanding the Constitution

The Constitutional Convention began in May 1787. On September 17, 1787, this document was written and signed by the congressional members of 12 of the 13 United States. Delegates from Rhode Island chose to leave the Continental Congress before the Constitution was completed. A total of 70 delegates were invited, 55 attended for some or all the convention. Thirty-nine of the delegates signed the Constitution of the United States. Nine months later, nine of the thirteen states had ratified the Constitution which made it the law of the land. Two hundred forty years have passed since that day, and only 27 Amendments have been added.

In the Federalist Papers, Madison wrote the Constitution was grounded on "the fundamental principles of the revolution...the transcendent laws of nature and of nature's God...the rights of humanity" which are addressed in the Declaration of Independence.[168]

The overall purpose of the Constitution is to give the Federal Government the power needed to run and protect the country while restraining it from becoming too powerful. Knowing that power corrupts human motivation, the Founders placed restraints on the authority of the federal government. The Constitution spells out exactly what the government is responsible for and places restraints on any other powers. All additional responsibilities belonged to the states. 'The People' can control the actions of the state government easier than the federal government.

---

[168] Alexander Hamilton et al., The Federalist (New York: New American Library, 1961), No. 39, 240; No. 40, 251; No. 43, 279-80.

Additionally, should we disapprove of a state's policies and can't effect change, we could leave the state as is happening in California now. If enough people and/or business leave one state for another, the state is forced to change or suffer the consequences. If the federal government becomes too powerful, the citizens can't leave for a better country—although many companies do.

The Framers of the Constitution limited the federal government by breaking it up into three separate entities or branches. The first is the Legislative branch which includes the House of Representatives and the Senate. The second is the Executive branch which includes the President. The third is the Judicial Branch or the Supreme Court.

The Founders believed by breaking up the powers of the federal government, chances of one branch becoming too powerful were minimized. Understanding the actions of men, they felt one branch would not relinquish their power to another branch—hence securing the three branches. Unfortunately, in this case, they were wrong. Congress, which represents the people have released much of their power and authority to both the President and the Supreme Court—essentially giving the people's power to a President and nine Justices.

This world-changing document begins with…

We the People of the United States, in Order to form a more perfect Union, establish Justice, insure domestic Tranquility, provide for the common defense, promote the general Welfare, and secure the Blessings of Liberty to ourselves and our Posterity, do ordain and establish this Constitution for the United States of America.

Establish Justice means: *to establish the virtue which consists in giving to everyone what is his due; practical conformity to the laws and to principles of rectitude in the dealings of men with each other; honesty; integrity in commerce or mutual intercourse.*[169]

---

[169]Webster, N. (1995). An American dictionary of the English language: an introductory dissertation of the origin, history and connection of the language of Western Asia, and of Europe and a concise grammar of the English language. San Francisco, CA: The Foundation for American Christian Education.

Domestic Tranquility means: *living at home with quietness; a calm state; freedom from disturbance or agitation.*

Posterity means: *all future generations of people.*[170]

The Founding Fathers placed a huge emphasis on "We the People" in the Constitution. As stated on the document itself, the words "We the People" are written about five times the size of the rest of the characters—making it clear this government will be run and controlled by the consent of the governed. The Framers placed checks and balances in place to assure this happens. Additionally, they placed a reset button (Article V), in case we the people allow our government to start controlling us instead of the people controlling the government (see How do we Repair the Nation, chapter 17).

The federal government's number one duty is to protect the freedom, liberty and rights of the American people—from terrorism, both foreign and domestic; riots and insurrections; and provide a military capable of protecting us in times of war.

"Promote the general welfare" doesn't mean the government is to set up welfare programs for the people. The Founders were compassionate people and believed in providing a safety net, not a living. Even this was meant more for the states to handle. In the preamble, general welfare refers to the federal government helping the states to operate together more efficiently. Some examples of this would be building interstate highways so people can get around more efficiently—or businesses could move products or services from state to state easier. Or perhaps, writing laws that allow insurance companies to compete in all states to give the people more competitive options for which to choose. The term is meant to provide for All the People. Not just the rich or just the poor. Not one race or social group over another. Not one type of business over another, such as funding for solar energy and de-promoting coal energy. I'll elaborate more when we study Article 1.

"Secure the blessings of liberty for ourselves and our posterity" means to assure the people have the right and option to govern themselves...the ability to make decisions in the best

---

[170] Webster, N. (1995). An American dictionary of the English language: an introductory dissertation of the origin, history and connection of the language of Western Asia, and of Europe and a concise grammar of the English language. San Francisco, CA: The Foundation for American Christian Education.

interest of their family. Liberty also means you must live with the benefits or consequences of your actions. The government is tasked to secure the blessings of liberty. So how does taking more of our money in the form of taxes, or requiring us to buy government-sponsored health care against our own will secure these liberties? They don't. The government has usurped our liberty while also reducing our ability to "pursue happiness."

So, to paraphrase this section: The People of the United States rein over the government. We concede a small amount of our liberty to the government for them to secure our borders, protect us from foreign and domestic enemies and establish justice for all people. While performing these duties, the government must not interfere with the American people's ability to pursue their God-given dreams and goals—utilizing the free enterprise system to capitalize on ideas and opportunities to provide the desired lifestyle for them and their family.

Chapter 11

Article I

Section 1

If our political system would enforce this first sentence of the first Article of the Constitution, half the problems with our government would probably disappear. There are countless books and articles written on this subject alone.

"All legislative Powers herein granted shall be vested in a Congress of the United States, which shall consist of a Senate and House of Representatives."

Congress is given the sole responsibility for making all laws, period. Presidential executive orders are not laws. The Environmental Protection Agency (EPA), The Internal Revenue Service (IRS), the United States Department of Health and Human Services (USFDA) or even the Department of Justice have zero constitutional authority in making or writing any kind of law. Yet many of our recent presidents, as well as the agencies mentioned above, exert their powers to enact laws which govern the people, industries, and businesses. This is illegal and unconstitutional and must end. (Please reference The Administrative State, Chapter 3)

The president and these governmental agencies are not the only groups of people illegally writing laws. The United States Supreme Court in addition to many of the lower courts are engaged in writing laws simply by misrepresenting the original intent of the Constitution to coincide with their political agenda (see Powers in Perspective, Chapter 1).

The Founders understood: for this republican democracy to survive, it is imperative for the people to elect men and women with high moral character and integrity. Without electing virtuous people, our government cannot stand. It will become corrupt, and the country will fall. These were concerns of our Founders, and long behold, they're coming true.

Corruption has become rampant. Recent and past presidents along with their 'administrative state' and many federal judges have established illegal laws, and Congress has allowed this to take place. They've conceded their power to the other branches instead of taking authority and putting an end to the misuse of power. Furthermore, the media is complicit with the government and skirting their First Amendment duties to inform the American people with the truth. They've become an arm of the progressive propaganda machine. Some examples of this are:

- The Affordable Care Act (Obamacare) forces Americans to buy a government-sponsored program—unconstitutional. The Supreme Court helped make the case by calling it a tax.
- Energy producing coal plants and coal mines are shutting down because of EPA regulations. Here the administrative state is making laws that affect the American people and business when these laws must first be written by our elected officials in Congress.
- Media bias example: The once respected New York Times Best Seller List is no longer "the best seller list." If you write a conservative book which sells more books than a progressive book, the progressive book will prevail as the leader on the list.

People are discouraged and uncertain as to what can be done. They're questioning whether their vote matters or who to trust. Part of the problem is, we've focused more on the vote for the President rather than the vote for our Congressman. Do you know who your House of Representative is? Many people don't. I'd venture to say the vote, and the scrutinizing of that vote for the House of Representatives are more important than the vote for the President. The Representative is the one person you have the most control over. We vote for them every two years and have the most access to them. They're the people walking in the local parades or having the local town hall meeting. They represent your interests in Washington. So, your vote must be based on a well-informed standpoint. When you go to court, you don't want the next lawyer in line—you want the best you can get to plead your case. This is no different. You want a representative that places the people in their district's best-interest first—a representative that understands the Constitution and will fight for our country's best interest. A well-informed vote for your representative is the foundation for the entire system to work properly.

Understanding of the Constitution is imperative to keeping our representatives from abusing the limited power we give them. For this reason, the progressive movement has worked hard to stop the teaching of the Constitution in schools. Knowing your rights will keep our politicians from overstepping their boundaries and less likely for them to become corrupt.

Section 2

The House of Representatives shall be composed of Members chosen every second Year by the People of the several States, and the Electors in each State shall have the Qualifications requisite for Electors of the most numerous Branch of the State Legislature.

No Person shall be a Representative who shall not have attained to the Age of twenty-five Years, and been seven Years a Citizen of the United States, and who shall not, when elected, be an Inhabitant of that State in which he shall be chosen.

Representatives and direct Taxes shall be apportioned among the several States which may be included within this Union, according to their respective Numbers, which shall be determined by adding to the whole Number of free Persons, including those bound to Service for a Term of Years, and excluding Indians not taxed, three fifths of all other Persons. The actual Enumeration shall be made within three Years after the first Meeting of the Congress of the United States, and within every subsequent Term of ten Years, in such Manner as they shall by Law direct. The Number of Representatives shall not exceed one for every thirty Thousand, but each State shall have at Least one Representative; and until such enumeration shall be made, the State of New Hampshire shall be entitled to choose three, Massachusetts eight, Rhode-Island and Providence

Plantations one, Connecticut five, New-York six, New Jersey four, Pennsylvania eight, Delaware one, Maryland six, Virginia ten, North Carolina five, South Carolina five, and Georgia three.

When vacancies happen in the Representation from any State, the Executive Authority thereof shall issue Writs of Election to fill such Vacancies.

The House of Representatives shall choose their Speaker and other Officers; and shall have the sole Power of Impeachment.

Article I, Section 2 pertains to the function of the House of Representatives. In a republican style government, the people are represented by a person of their choosing. This section describes the guidelines for choosing the representative. First, they must run for re-election every two years. The Founders established this policy to keep the representative as close to the people as possible. If we're not satisfied with them, we can replace them after two years. After Election Day, they'll perform their duties as our representative for maybe a year and a half before they start campaigning again. Since we tend to have short memories, this keeps them true to their word; otherwise, they won't be re-elected. Of course, this also assumes the American People are doing their job and paying attention to each representative's voting record and actions.

Think of it this way. As parents, if we let our young children do anything they choose to and ignore their behavior, would they correct themselves—of course not. Our politicians aren't any different, unfettered they will run rampant. Each representative should be aware of how their policies affect the lives of their constituents.

The Constitution states that the House of Representatives is the *"most numerous Branch of the Legislature."* The number of representatives is determined by the population of a state. For every thirty thousand people, there will be one representative. Doing the math, in 1789, there would be a total of sixty-five Representatives in Congress. Today, our population is almost 325 million people which means Congress should have over ten thousand eight hundred Representatives in Washington, D.C.

However, in 1929 Congress passed an act that limited the number of representatives to four hundred thirty-five. Therefore, today we essentially have one representative per every seven-hundred-forty-seven thousand people. Can one person represent that many people? Certainly not—and another example of why removing power from Washington, D.C. and returning it to the states is critical.

The representative must be at least twenty-five years old and a citizen of America for at least seven years. As America's population continued to grow, the Founders wanted any new immigrants to be citizens for at least seven years. This gave them time to assimilate into the American culture.

In calculating the number of people in each state, Indians were excluded because they weren't required to pay taxes and slaves were counted as three fifths—or three head counts per every five slaves. This reduced the power of states that promoted slavery. However, states could increase the number of representatives in Congress (thus increasing their power), simply by freeing their slaves.

Section 2, then talks about the *"the actual enumeration"* or census as it is called today. Each state had to conduct an election within three years of the first meeting of Congress after the signing of the Constitution and then every ten years after that.

The House of Representatives would choose their Speaker or leader. They will also have the sole power of impeachment—which means 'to accuse of unlawful activity.' If the president or another government official acted unlawfully, the House, which is "closest to the people" could impeach the official and then present their case to the Senate.

Section 3
The Senate of the United States shall be composed of two Senators from each State, chosen by the Legislature thereof, for six Years; and each Senator shall have one Vote.
Immediately after they shall be assembled in Consequence of the first Election, they shall be divided as equally as may be into three Classes. The Seats of the Senators of the first Class shall be vacated at the Expiration of the second Year, of the second Class at the Expiration of the fourth Year, and of the third Class at the Expiration of the sixth Year, so that one third may be chosen every second Year; and if Vacancies

happen by Resignation, or otherwise, during the Recess of the Legislature of any State, the Executive thereof may make temporary Appointments until the next Meeting of the Legislature, which shall then fill such Vacancies.

No Person shall be a Senator who shall not have attained to the Age of thirty Years, and been nine Years a Citizen of the United States, and who shall not, when elected, be an Inhabitant of that State for which he shall be chosen.

The Vice President of the United States shall be President of the Senate, but shall have no Vote, unless they be equally divided.

The Senate shall choose their other Officers, and also a President pro tempore, in the Absence of the Vice President, or when he shall exercise the Office of President of the United States.

The Senate shall have the sole Power to try all Impeachments. When sitting for that Purpose, they shall be on Oath or Affirmation. When the President of the United States is tried, the Chief Justice shall preside: And no Person shall be convicted without the Concurrence of two thirds of the Members present.

Judgment in Cases of Impeachment shall not extend further than to removal from Office, and disqualification to hold and enjoy any Office of honor, Trust or Profit under the United States: but the Party convicted shall nevertheless be liable and subject to Indictment, Trial, Judgment and Punishment, according to Law.

The first sentence of this section, *"The Senate of the United States shall be composed of two Senators from each State, chosen by the Legislature thereof, for six Years"* has changed. Today we still have two Senators per state. However, on May 13, 1912, Congress passed the 17th Amendment, and the states ratified it on April 8, 1913, which changed who should choose the Senators. Originally, the legislature from each state would choose two Senators to represent them in Washington. Today the people of each state vote for the two Senators for their state (See the 17th Amendment, chapter 16, for additional comments).

In the Federalist Papers No. 62 & No. 63, James Madison discusses five reasons for a Senate and how they are chosen. We will cover these five points when we discuss the 17th Amendment.

The progressive era led to changing this section to usurp some of the power and authority from the state and in essence, giving the federal government more control.

Since there are two Senators per state, there will always be the possibility of a tie vote. So, the Founders put this provision in the Constitution: The Vice President of the United States shall be President of the Senate but shall have no Vote, unless they are equally divided.

Section 4

The Times, Places and Manner of holding Elections for Senators and Representatives, shall be prescribed in each State by the Legislature thereof; but the Congress may at any time by Law make or alter such Regulations, except as to the Places of choosing Senators.

The Congress shall assemble at least once in every Year, and such Meeting shall be on the first Monday in December, unless they shall by Law appoint a different Day.

Each state has the right to choose the time, places and way the elections are being held but Congress may change the time by law. In 1845, Congress did pass a law making it the first Tuesday after the first Monday in November.

Congress was required to assemble at least once per year. The day and time for the first annual meeting of the year were changed by the second section of the XX amendment of the Constitution to January 3rd at 12:00 noon. This amendment was passed by Congress on March 2, 1932, and ratified by the states on January 23, 1933.

Section 5

Each House shall be the Judge of the Elections, Returns and Qualifications of its own Members, and a Majority of each shall constitute a Quorum to do Business; but a smaller Number may adjourn from day to day, and may be authorized to compel the Attendance of absent Members, in such Manner, and under such Penalties as each House may provide.

Each House may determine the Rules of its Proceedings, punish its Members for disorderly Behavior, and, with the Concurrence of two thirds, expel a Member.

Each House shall keep a Journal of its Proceedings, and from time to time publish the same, excepting such Parts as may in their Judgment require Secrecy; and the Yeas and Nays of the Members of either House on any question shall, at the Desire of one fifth of those Present, be entered on the Journal.

Neither House, during the Session of Congress, shall, without the Consent of the other, adjourn for more than three days, nor to any other Place than that in which the two Houses shall be sitting.

Quorum means: *A bench of justices or such a number of officers or members as is competent by law or constitution to transact business.*[171]

Section 5 has several key points to address. First, for the House of Representatives and the Senate to conduct business, a majority of the Congressmen must be present—half the members plus one.

The second key point is the Senate, and the House must keep a journal of its proceedings. This allows the people to reference the "original intent" of any bill which was passed especially when hundreds of years later times and terms have changed. Today the first and second amendments are under attack by the progressive movement (Our rights to free speech and to bear arms). Knowing the original intent of our Founders can be investigated because they kept journals.

Thirdly, the votes of each member are recorded and of public record so 'We the People' may know how our representatives have voted.

The final key point is one house of Congress cannot adjourn for more than three days without the consent of the other House. If important legislation needs to be addressed, both houses must be available. This will prevent one house adjourning as a political move to avoid dealing with the issue. King George was

---

[171] Webster, N. (1995). An American dictionary of the English language: an introductory dissertation of the origin, history and connection of the language of Western Asia, and of Europe and a concise grammar of the English language. San Francisco, CA: The Foundation for American Christian Education.

notorious for this kind of action as described in the Declaration of Independence under grievance number 2.

Section 6
The Senators and Representatives shall receive a Compensation for their Services, to be ascertained by Law, and paid out of the Treasury of the United States. They shall in all Cases, except Treason, Felony and Breach of the Peace, be privileged from Arrest during their Attendance at the Session of their respective Houses, and in going to and returning from the same; and for any Speech or Debate in either House, they shall not be questioned in any other Place. No Senator or Representative shall, during the Time for which he was elected, be appointed to any civil Office under the Authority of the United States, which shall have been created, or the Emoluments whereof shall have been increased during such time; and no Person holding any Office under the United States, shall be a Member of either House during his Continuance in Office.

Definition of Emoluments means: *The profit arising from office or employment; that which is received as a compensation for services, or which is annexed to the possession of office, as salary, fees and perquisites.*

Members of Congress will be paid for serving our country. They cannot be arrested while traveling to or from Congress or while in session except for treason, a felony or breach of peace. They cannot hold any other office in government while they are serving in Congress.

Section 7
All Bills for raising Revenue shall originate in the House of Representatives; but the Senate may propose or concur with Amendments as on other Bills.
Every Bill which shall have passed the House of Representatives and the Senate, shall, before it become a Law, be presented to the President of the United States; If he approve he shall sign it, but if not he shall return it, with his Objections to that House in which it shall have originated, who shall enter the Objections at large on their Journal, and

proceed to reconsider it. If after such Reconsideration two thirds of that House shall agree to pass the Bill, it shall be sent, together with the Objections, to the other House, by which it shall likewise be reconsidered, and if approved by two thirds of that House, it shall become a Law. But in all such Cases the Votes of both Houses shall be determined by yeas and Nays, and the Names of the Persons voting for and against the Bill shall be entered on the Journal of each House respectively. If any Bill shall not be returned by the President within ten Days (Sundays excepted) after it shall have been presented to him, the Same shall be a Law, in like Manner as if he had signed it, unless the Congress by their Adjournment prevent its Return, in which Case it shall not be a Law.

Every Order, Resolution, or Vote to which the Concurrence of the Senate and House of Representatives may be necessary (except on a question of Adjournment) shall be presented to the President of the United States; and before the Same shall take Effect, shall be approved by him, or being disapproved by him, shall be repassed by two thirds of the Senate and House of Representatives, according to the Rules and Limitations prescribed in the Case of a Bill.

Section 7 details the process for passing a bill in Congress. Since the House of Representatives controls the purse for this country, all bills requiring the raising of money from the people must originate from the House of Representatives. A majority vote from each House of Congress will send the bill to the President for signing. If he signs the bill, it becomes law. Should he decide not to sign the bill and sends it back to Congress—the House and Senate can make any suggested changes by the President and return it to him for signing or pass it with a two-thirds vote from each house, it then becomes law without the President's signature. Should the President not return the bill within ten days it becomes law unless Congress had adjourned. (A side note, this is a resolution to grievance number 17 in the Declaration of Independence)

Section 8
The Congress shall have Power To lay and collect Taxes, Duties, Imposts and Excises, to pay the Debts and provide for the common Defense and general Welfare of the United

States; but all Duties, Imposts and Excises shall be uniform throughout the United States;

To borrow Money on the credit of the United States;

To regulate Commerce with foreign Nations, and among the several States, and with the Indian Tribes;

To establish an uniform Rule of Naturalization, and uniform Laws on the subject of Bankruptcies throughout the United States;

To coin Money, regulate the Value thereof, and of foreign Coin, and fix the Standard of Weights and Measures;

To provide for the Punishment of counterfeiting the Securities and current Coin of the United States;

To establish Post Offices and post Roads;

To promote the Progress of Science and useful Arts, by securing for limited Times to Authors and Inventors the exclusive Right to their respective Writings and Discoveries;

To constitute Tribunals inferior to the Supreme Court;

To define and punish Piracies and Felonies committed on the high Seas, and Offences against the Law of Nations;

To declare War, grant Letters of Marque and Reprisal, and make Rules concerning Captures on Land and Water;

To raise and support Armies, but no Appropriation of Money to that Use shall be for a longer Term than two Years;

To provide and maintain a Navy;

To make Rules for the Government and Regulation of the land and naval Forces;

To provide for calling forth the Militia to execute the Laws of the Union, suppress Insurrections and repel Invasions;

To provide for organizing, arming, and disciplining, the Militia, and for governing such Part of them as may be employed in the Service of the United States, reserving to the States respectively, the Appointment of the Officers, and the Authority of training the Militia according to the discipline prescribed by Congress;

To exercise exclusive Legislation in all Cases whatsoever, over such District (not exceeding ten Miles square) as may, by Cession of particular States, and the Acceptance of Congress, become the Seat of the Government of the United States, and to exercise like Authority over all Places

purchased by the Consent of the Legislature of the State in which the Same shall be, for the Erection of Forts, Magazines, Arsenals, dock-Yards, and other needful Buildings; —And To make all Laws which shall be necessary and proper for carrying into Execution the foregoing Powers, and all other Powers vested by this Constitution in the Government of the United States, or in any Department or Officer thereof.

Welfare means: 1. *When applied to person—Exemption from misfortune, sickness, calamity or evil; the enjoyment of health and the common blessing of life; prosperity; happiness; 2. When applied to states—Exemption from any unusual evil or calamity; the enjoyment of peace and prosperity, or ordinary blessings of society and civil government.*

Naturalization means: *The act of investing an alien with the rights and privileges of a native subject or citizen. It is by act of Congress, vesting certain tribunals with the power.*

Militia means: *The body of soldiers in a state enrolled for discipline, but not engaged in actual service except in emergencies: as distinguished from regular troop, whose sole occupation is war or military service.*

Section 8 lists specific powers given to Congress most of which is straight forward. Although, there are a few items worth noting—for example *The Congress shall have Power To...and provide for the common Defense and general Welfare of the United States;* Aside from slavery, at no point in the Constitution do the Founder speak of a provision which pertains to any individual or class of individuals. It speaks of the federal government or to the 'states' as a whole. Congress has the power to provide for the common defense and general welfare of the—United States. Congress does not have the power to raise taxes to pay for individual welfare. This was another progressive over-reach during the mid-1900s. Helping individuals is the responsibility of the states, not the federal government.

Another area that has been distorted by the progressive movement is: *To promote the Progress of Science and useful Arts, by securing for limited Times to Authors and Inventors the exclusive Right to their respective Writings and Discoveries;* The National Endowment for the Arts, a government agency, part of the administrative state, has spent well over ten billion dollars of tax payer's money just since 1966. Taxpayer dollars are funding these groups that should not be allowed.

Stating again, knowing the original intent of the Constitution is critical. The Founders wanted to promote the progress of science and useful arts "by" securing authors and inventors exclusive rights with U.S. patents. In other words, they wanted to protect the authors and inventors from having other people pirate their ideas while making a profit with it. They wanted to protect free enterprise in our country. Unfortunately, the government has distorted this section by acting as if the Constitution just states: To promote the Progress of Science and useful Arts.

The Founders argued heavily about having a standing army and navy (see grievance numbers 11 & 12 in the Declaration of Independence). At first thought, you might ask why that would even be an issue. After reading their arguments you understand, they were concerned about Liberty. History proved many times over; a tyrant has had the power to smooth over the military leaders and usurped the military into helping them eliminate the republic and become a dictatorship. Two examples of this are the Roman Empire and the King of England.

The Founders decided to go ahead and maintain a standing army and navy with two important controls: First, Congress would control the purse which paid them. This was important because the Congressmen were closest to the people; second, they would maintain a militia where the people were allowed to keep and bear arms. This way if the President were to take command of the military in a manner of becoming a dictator, the people would still have a way of defending their freedom.

Congress has control over a ten-mile square piece of property called the District of Columbia or better known as Washington, D.C. This land was part of Maryland and part of Virginia. The Founders called this land "Federal Town," but the Anti-Federalist referred to it as "a sink of corruption and a potential nursery for tyrants."

Lastly, Congress can make laws that assist in the proper execution of the powers given them by Article I section 8 of the Constitution.

Section 9

The Migration or Importation of such Persons as any of the States now existing shall think proper to admit, shall not be prohibited by the Congress prior to the Year one thousand eight hundred and eight, but a Tax or duty may be imposed on such Importation, not exceeding ten dollars for each Person.

The Privilege of the Writ of Habeas Corpus shall not be suspended, unless when in Cases of Rebellion or Invasion the public Safety may require it.

No Bill of Attainder or ex post facto Law shall be passed.

No Capitation, or other direct, Tax shall be laid, unless in Proportion to the Census or enumeration herein before directed to be taken.

No Tax or Duty shall be laid on Articles exported from any State.

No Preference shall be given by any Regulation of Commerce or Revenue to the Ports of one State over those of another: nor shall Vessels bound to, or from, one State, be obliged to enter, clear, or pay Duties in another.

No Money shall be drawn from the Treasury, but in Consequence of Appropriations made by Law; and a regular Statement and Account of the Receipts and Expenditures of all public Money shall be published from time to time.

No Title of Nobility shall be granted by the United States: And no Person holding any Office of Profit or Trust under them, shall, without the Consent of the Congress, accept of any present, Emolument, Office, or Title, of any kind whatever, from any King, Prince, or foreign State.

Notice section 8 is a list of items Congress <u>can</u> do and section 9 is a list of items Congress <u>cannot</u> do. The first key item in this section is: *The Migration or Importation of such Persons as any of the States now existing shall think proper to admit, shall not be prohibited by the Congress prior to the Year one thousand eight hundred and eight, but a Tax or duty may be imposed on such Importation, not exceeding ten dollars for each Person.*

This is the slavery argument. Eleven of the states did not want slavery. Gouverneur Morris called slavery a "Nefarious institution" and "the curse of Heaven." George Mason condemned it and called it "infernal traffic" and Luther Martin argued that it was "inconsistent with the principles of the Revolution and dishonorable to the American character." James Iredell explained the clause as follows:

> *"For my part, were it practicable to put an end to the importation of slaves immediately, it would give me the greatest pleasure; for it certainly is a trade utterly inconsistent with the rights of humanity, and under which great cruelties have been exercised. When the entire abolition of slavery takes place, it will be an event which must be pleasing to every generous mind and every friend of human nature; but we often wish for things which are not attainable. It was the wish of an overwhelming majority of the Convention to put an end to the trade immediately; but the states of South Carolina and Georgia would not agree to it."*

The compromise was for the slave clause to be in place till 1808. Both sides of the argument hoped the other side would soften their resolve. The compromise included proper wording such as 'moral persons' instead of "slaves or property' in an effort to recognize them as such. On January 1, 1808, Congress passed, and President Jefferson signed into law, a federal prohibition of the importation of slaves to the United States. This was the first day it could be addressed—becoming the beginning of the end of slavery.

Congress cannot suspend the Writ of Habeas corpus which means they can't stop the people from filing a claim stating someone is imprisoned unlawfully unless it's due to rebellion or invasion. Congress cannot pass a bill of attainder which declares a person or group guilty without a trial. Congress cannot pass ex post facto laws which mean to pass a law after an action or crime was committed in order to charge the person with the illegal action or crime when at the time it wasn't illegal. No preference shall be given to one state over another. No money may be used by Congress that has not been authorized by law.

Section 10

No State shall enter into any Treaty, Alliance, or Confederation; grant Letters of Marque and Reprisal; coin Money; emit Bills of Credit; make any Thing but gold and silver Coin a Tender in Payment of Debts; pass any Bill of Attainder, ex post facto Law, or Law impairing the Obligation of Contracts, or grant any Title of Nobility.

No State shall, without the Consent of the Congress, lay any Imposts or Duties on Imports or Exports, except what may be absolutely necessary for executing it's inspection Laws: and the net Produce of all Duties and Imposts, laid by any State on Imports or Exports, shall be for the Use of the Treasury of the United States; and all such Laws shall be subject to the Revision and Control of the Congress.

No State shall, without the Consent of Congress, lay any Duty of Tonnage, keep Troops, or Ships of War in time of Peace, enter into any Agreement or Compact with another State, or with a foreign Power, or engage in War, unless actually invaded, or in such imminent Danger as will not admit of delay.

Section 10 identifies rules the states must abide by—they are <u>not</u> allowed to do. They are items which Congress is responsible for, or neither Congress nor the state is permitted to do.

Chapter 12

Article II

Section 1

The executive Power shall be vested in a President of the United States of America. He shall hold his Office during the Term of four Years, and, together with the Vice President, chosen for the same Term, be elected, as follows

Each State shall appoint, in such Manner as the Legislature thereof may direct, a Number of Electors, equal to the whole Number of Senators and Representatives to which the State may be entitled in the Congress: but no Senator or Representative, or Person holding an Office of Trust or Profit under the United States, shall be appointed an Elector. The Electors shall meet in their respective States, and vote by Ballot for two Persons, of whom one at least shall not be an Inhabitant of the same State with themselves. And they shall make a List of all the Persons voted for, and of the Number of Votes for each; which List they shall sign and certify and transmit sealed to the Seat of the Government of the United States, directed to the President of the Senate. The President of the Senate shall, in the Presence of the Senate and House of Representatives, open all the Certificates, and the Votes shall then be counted. The Person having the greatest Number of Votes shall be the President, if such Number be a Majority of the whole Number of Electors appointed; and if there be more than one who have such Majority, and have an equal Number of Votes, then the House of Representatives shall immediately choose by Ballot one of them for President; and if no Person have a Majority, then from the five highest on the List the said House shall in like Manner choose the President.

But in choosing the President, the Votes shall be taken by States, the Representation from each State having one Vote; A quorum for this Purpose shall consist of a Member or Members from two thirds of the States, and a Majority of all the States shall be necessary to a Choice. In every Case, after the Choice of the President, the Person having the greatest Number of Votes of the Electors shall be the Vice President. But if there should remain two or more who have equal Votes, the Senate shall choose from them by Ballot the Vice President.

The President is the Executive of the United States. He's responsible for enforcing all laws of the land. The Executive Power given to the President is used as a tool for assisting his efforts in executing the laws on the books both foreign and domestic.

He is elected to a four-year term (with a maximum of two terms per the XXII Amendment of the Constitution). The President is elected by receiving the greatest number of electoral votes. Each state is given a number of electoral votes based on the number of legislators they have. For example, Ohio has sixteen House of Representatives and two Senators. Therefore, Ohio has eighteen electoral votes.

Prior to the ratification of the 12th amendment and then superseded by the 20th amendment, each elector shall vote for two people. These votes shall be sealed and sent to Congress where the President of the Senate (The Vice President) shall open the sealed votes in front of the House and the Senate. These votes are then counted. The person with the most votes will be the next President of the United States and the person with the second most votes will be the next Vice President. Should a tie for the President occur, then the House of Representatives chooses the President. If there is a tie vote for the Vice President than the Senate chooses the Vice President.

The Congress may determine the Time of choosing the Electors, and the Day on which they shall give their Votes; which Day shall be the same throughout the United States.

No Person except a natural born Citizen, or a Citizen of the United States, at the time of the Adoption of this Constitution, shall be eligible to the Office of President; neither shall any Person be eligible to that Office who shall not have attained

to the Age of thirty five Years, and been fourteen Years a Resident within the United States.
The Constitution states several qualifications which must be met in order to run for the office of the President of the United States. They are as follows:

- The person must be a natural born citizen or a citizen prior to the ratification of the Constitution.
- Must be at least thirty-five years old.
- Must have been a resident of the United States for at least 14 years.
- Today, to legally run for the office of the President you must be a natural born citizen and at least age 35.

In Case of the Removal of the President from Office, or of his Death, Resignation, or Inability to discharge the Powers and Duties of the said Office, the Same shall devolve on the Vice President, and the Congress may by Law provide for the Case of Removal, Death, Resignation or Inability, both of the President and Vice President, declaring what Officer shall then act as President, and such Officer shall act accordingly, until the Disability be removed, or a President shall be elected.
If the President of the United States is unable to perform his duties as President, Congress has the power to remove him from office and give the duties to the Vice President until the said disability or circumstance is removed. If the Vice President cannot perform the duties of the President, then the position is passed on to the Speaker of the House of Representatives.
The President shall, at stated Times, receive for his Services, a Compensation, which shall neither be increased nor diminished during the Period for which he shall have been elected, and he shall not receive within that Period any other Emolument from the United States, or any of them.
The President shall be paid for his services. This salary shall not be increased or decreased during his elected tenure. In other words, he cannot raise his salary while in office. He may request a pay raise for the next President and if passed by Congress than the next President may receive that pay raise. If

he's then re-elected, he may receive that pay. He may receive no other emolument (advantage, benefit, profit or wage for being employed as President).

Before he enter on the Execution of his Office, he shall take the following Oath or Affirmation: —"I do solemnly swear (or affirm) that I will faithfully execute the Office of President of the United States, and will to the best of my Ability, preserve, protect and defend the Constitution of the United States."

Repeating the key line in this portion of the Constitution: —"*I do solemnly swear (or affirm) that I will faithfully execute the Office of President of the United States, and will to the best of my Ability, preserve, protect and defend the Constitution of the United States.*" Knowing the Constitution assures America of her liberty. If the President is NOT faithfully preserving, protecting and defending the Constitution of the United States, we will know it. Over the years, many Presidents have used executive orders to by-pass Congress. They make what amounts to a "temporary law" which we must abide by. Temporary, since it did not come from Congress, the next President can change it with his own executive order.

The President is to preserve and protect the Constitution as it is written. All too often, when we hear the President defending the Constitution, it's for political expediency—or they're picking and choosing which laws to defend and ignoring ones they disagree with. The President took an oath to preserve, protect and defend the Constitution. There is nothing vague about this statement. If the President disagrees with it, he can use his powerful bully pulpit to seek change in the law, but in the meantime, he's required to defend it.

Section 2

The President shall be Commander in Chief of the Army and Navy of the United States, and of the Militia of the several States, when called into the actual Service of the United States; he may require the Opinion, in writing, of the principal Officer in each of the executive Departments, upon any Subject relating to the Duties of their respective Offices, and he shall have Power to grant Reprieves and Pardons for Offences against the United States, except in Cases of Impeachment.

The President is the Commander in Chief of the Army and Navy of the United States, along with the Militia of several states. At that time, there wasn't an Air Force or Coast Guard, but there was a Militia. The second amendment mentions the militia. We'll discuss militia then. For now, the President is in charge of the militia assuming he's not part of a coup attempting to usurp our freedom.

He shall have Power, by and with the Advice and Consent of the Senate, to make Treaties, provided two thirds of the Senators present concur; and he shall nominate, and by and with the Advice and Consent of the Senate, shall appoint Ambassadors, other public Ministers and Consuls, Judges of the supreme Court, and all other Officers of the United States, whose Appointments are not herein otherwise provided for, and which shall be established by Law: but the Congress may by Law vest the Appointment of such inferior Officers, as they think proper, in the President alone, in the Courts of Law, or in the Heads of Departments.

The President's power includes making treaties with other countries, but he must have approval from two-thirds of the Senate. His powers also consist of the appointments of Supreme Court and Federal Judges, Ambassadors for the U.S., heads of departments and other senior officers. However, Congress must approve these appointments.

The President shall have the Power to fill up all Vacancies that may happen during the Recess of the Senate, by granting Commissions which shall expire at the End of their next Session.

The Framers gave the President this power to keep the country running properly while the Senate was at recess. Back in the late 1700s, early 1800s Congress may have only convened once a year. They'd come back on horseback because there were no cars or planes at that time. They would attend to any business needs and issues which may take from three to six months then get back on their horse or buggy and head back home to their state. Congress may not reconvene again till the following year. Today this clause is unnecessary because Congress can convene at a given notice to attend to any pressing business necessary. Today, the President has used this clause to make appointments that otherwise the Senate would have rejected. The President waits till Congress goes out on recess then make what's called a "Recessed appointment." If this practice continues, we may need a future amendment to restore order.

Section 3
He shall from time to time give to the Congress Information of the State of the Union, and recommend to their Consideration such Measures as he shall judge necessary and expedient; he may, on extraordinary Occasions, convene both Houses, or either of them, and in Case of Disagreement between them, with Respect to the Time of Adjournment, he may adjourn them to such Time as he shall think proper; he shall receive Ambassadors and other public Ministers; he shall take Care that the Laws be faithfully executed, and shall Commission all the Officers of the United States.

A couple of key points from this are: First, every January the President gives his State of the Union address to Congress. Secondly, the Founders re-stated the President is to "take Care that the Laws be faithfully executed." Mentioning it in section 1 and again in section 3 should indicate a strong emphasis on this law.

Section 4
The President, Vice President and all civil Officers of the United States, shall be removed from Office on Impeachment for, and Conviction of, Treason, Bribery, or other high Crimes and Misdemeanors.

As discussed in the last chapter, the House of Representatives have the sole power to impeach any of the officers mentioned above, and the Senate has the sole power to try these officers of the crime.

Chapter 13

Article III

The third leg of government outlined in the Constitution is the Judicial Branch covered in Article III beginning with the Supreme Court. Many of the Founders were lawyers and had plenty of experience with the court systems in England. Witnessing their actions first hand, the Founders knew this leg must be contained otherwise they would subvert the will of the people.

Article III has many words and terms not commonly used today. Here are some of their definitions:

Inferior Courts: *There are many types of Federal Courts which fall under the high court, the Supreme Court. Several include the U.S. Court of Appeals and then the U.S. District Courts. These courts are established by Congress under Article I Section 8 of the Constitution.*

Good behavior: *This term is assumed to mean the Federal Judges are appointed to the bench for life as long as they act in good behavior.*

Equity means: *Justice; right. In practice, equity is the impartial distribution of justice, or the doing that to another which the laws of God and man, and of reason, give him a right to claim.*

Ambassadors, other Public Ministers and Consuls are: In Noah Webster's 1828 dictionary, he states that the word ambassador is the more common spelling, but he states, *"good authors write Embassador." A minister of the highest rank employed by one prince or state, at the court of another, to manage the public concerns of his own prince or state and representing the power and dignity of his sovereign.*

Bill of Attainder: *This is a legislative act finding a person guilty of treason or a felony without a trial.*

Corruption of Blood: *This was part of an ancient English penalty for treason. It was usually part of a Bill of Attainder, which normally sentenced the accused to death. The corruption of blood would forbid the accused's family from inheriting his property. Such bills and punishments were often inflicted upon Tories by colonial governments immediately following independence.*

Tories: *In America, during the Revolution, those who opposed the war, and favored the claims of Great Britain.*

Admiralty means: *The Supreme Court in England for the trial of maritime causes. In the United States, there is no admiralty court, distinct from others; but the district courts, established in the several states by Congress, are invested with admiralty powers.*

Section 1
The Judicial Power of the United States shall be vested in one Supreme Court and in such inferior Courts as the Congress may from time to time ordain and establish. The Judges, both of the supreme and inferior Courts, shall hold their Offices during good Behavior, and shall, at stated Times, receive for their Services, a Compensation, which shall not be diminished during their Continuance in Office.

The Constitution gives certain powers to the judges to rule in a court of law. The Supreme Court is the highest court in the land, and Congress can appoint inferior courts as they see fit.

The 9th grievance against the King of England listed on the Declaration of Independence describes how the King would influence the judges by threatening their jobs and salaries if they made decisions against the King's best interest. This influenced the Founders to put the above clause giving the judges a permanent job with a permanent salary. The Founders felt this would protect the American people from judges being influenced by political pressures. Alexander Hamilton wrote in The Federalist No. 78: *"judges must follow the Constitution instead of a clearly contrary ordinary law."* The judges must make their decisions based on the original intent of the Constitution regardless of whether Congress passes other laws that may affect their decision. Whether the President signed an executive order or Congress passed a law, the judges must not be influenced in any way.

During the late 1700s and early 1800s, the life expectancy of Americans was about 59 years old. Today it's closer to 79 years old. When the Founders set the term of a judge based on good behavior, they didn't expect judges to remain on the bench well into their 70's and 80's. According to stats from Wikipedia the average Supreme Court Justice from 1789-1970 were on the bench 14.9 years. Today they average 25.6 years. From 1789-1970 a new judge was appointed to the Bench every 1.91 years. Today that number is 3.75 years. These facts make a compelling case for a judicial term limits amendment to the Constitution.

The Founders appointed Congress to determine the number of judges sitting on the Supreme Court. Over the years this number has changed based mostly on political posturing. Congress originally set the number to six Supreme Court Judges in 1789. In 1801 they reduced it to five judges to keep incoming President Thomas Jefferson from appointing a judge when one of the judges was getting ready to retire. Then in 1802, Congress raised it back up to six. During the Civil War, Congress expanded the number to ten judges to help President Abraham Lincoln. Later, it was back down to seven to deprive President Andrew Johnson of making Supreme Court selections. In 1869, Congress set the number at nine where it has remained despite an attempt by President Franklin D. Roosevelt to increase the number of judges to assist his political agenda.

Section 2
The judicial Power shall extend to all Cases, in Law and Equity, arising under this Constitution, the Laws of the United States, and Treaties made, or which shall be made, under their Authority;—to all Cases affecting Ambassadors, other public Ministers and Consuls;—to all Cases of admiralty and maritime Jurisdiction;—to Controversies to which the United States shall be a Party;—to Controversies between two or more States;— between a State and Citizens of another State,—between Citizens of different States,—between Citizens of the same State claiming Lands under Grants of

different States, and between a State, or the Citizens thereof, and foreign States, Citizens or Subjects.

In all Cases affecting Ambassadors, other public Ministers and Consuls, and those in which a State shall be Party, the Supreme Court shall have original Jurisdiction. In all the other Cases before mentioned, the Supreme Court shall have appellate Jurisdiction, both as to Law and Fact, with such Exceptions, and under such Regulations as the Congress shall make.

The Trial of all Crimes, except in Cases of Impeachment, shall be by Jury; and such Trial shall be held in the State where the said Crimes shall have been committed; but when not committed within any State, the Trial shall be at such Place or Places as the Congress may by Law have directed.

The Constitution was designed to be a limiting document to protect our freedom and liberty. This section lists very specific responsibilities—omitting nothing. Therefore, our federal courts should not be ruling on cases which don't fall under the above-listed jurisdiction. (Section 2 is the answer to the grievance 18 in the Declaration of Independence).

Section 3

Treason against the United States shall consist only in levying War against them, or in adhering to their Enemies, giving them Aid and Comfort. No Person shall be convicted of Treason unless on the Testimony of two Witnesses to the same overt Act, or on Confession in open Court.

The Congress shall have Power to declare the Punishment of Treason, but no Attainder of Treason shall work Corruption of Blood, or Forfeiture except during the Life of the Person attainted.

Section 2 and 3 list the extent and scope of the Federal Court Judges' jurisdiction and the responsibilities they have regarding the Constitution. All Federal Judges must know the Constitution and pass their judgment based on the original intent of the Founders—or the original intent of any of the Amendments. They're never permitted to make judgments based on political views or on the change in times. Their decisions should never affect laws on the books unless it's the law itself; they are deciding whether it is constitutional or not.

Charles Warren, Lawyer, and author wrote a three-volume set of books called "The Supreme Court in United States History." He's quoted as saying *however the Court may interpret the provisions of the Constitution, it is still the Constitution which is the law, not the decisions of the Court."* Supreme Court Judge Antonin Scalia recently passed away. He was one of a few judges still on the court which made decisions based on the original intent of the Constitution. It is imperative to our freedom and liberty that "We the People" know and understand the Constitution—and hold our politicians accountable for selecting judges with high moral character and integrity. In the Anti-Federalist Papers number XI, Brutus expresses his concern on the power of the Supreme Court; he writes: *"This power in the judicial will enable them to mold the government, into almost any shape they please."*

Article III doesn't give the Supreme Court the power to make laws—or interpret the Constitution as it sees fit. Nor does it give the Supreme Court the authority to rule based on political spin.

For example, the Supreme Court didn't have the authority to rule that a baby in a womb is not a real person and therefore, it can be aborted. However, our elected officials in Congress do have the authority to write legislation to protect a fetus simply by claiming life begins at conception. This law would overrule the court's decision. But that requires the American people to vote men and women into Congress with strong character and virtue.

The Supreme Court wasn't given the authority to rule that God is no longer allowed in the public square. These are all ideas to promote the progressive agenda. If the ruling on these two cases, and others, were based on the original intent of the Constitution and the intentions of the Founders, the outcomes would have been different.

When going to the ballot box, are you aware of the judges you will be voting for? I hope after reading this book, you will research before selecting a candidate, and every decision you make is an informed decision. Our country is counting on you. Your children and grandchildren are counting on you.

George Washington: Picture was taken at Valley Forge, Pa.

Chapter 14

Article IV

Section 1
Full Faith and Credit shall be given in each State to the public Acts, Records, and judicial Proceedings of every other State. And the Congress may by general Laws prescribe the Manner in which such Acts, Records and Proceedings shall be proved, and the Effect thereof.

Article IV concerns the relationship between the federal government and the states—and the relationship of one state to another. Section 1 deal with the creditworthiness of one state to another—and one citizen to another state across state borders. It includes the judicial court decisions made in one state being honored by another state. This could be where same-sex marriage and the defense of marriage act meet regarding the Constitution.

Section 2
The Citizens of each State shall be entitled to all Privileges and Immunities of Citizens in the several States.
A Person charged in any State with Treason, Felony, or other Crime, who shall flee from Justice, and be found in another State, shall on Demand of the executive Authority of the State from which he fled, be delivered up, to be removed to the State having Jurisdiction of the Crime.
No Person held to Service or Labor in one State, under the Laws thereof, escaping into another, shall, in Consequence of any Law or Regulation therein, be discharged from such Service or Labor, but shall be delivered up on Claim of the Party to whom such Service or Labor may be due.

This section allows the sharing of privileges and immunities allotted to free men—and criminal extradition if some criminal runs to another state they can be arrested and sent back to the state where the crime was committed. This also includes the slave clause stating if a slave ran from one state, he would be arrested and brought back to the state where he was serving. I'll address this in more detail when we discuss the 13th amendment to the Constitution where all slaves were set free.

Section 3
New States may be admitted by the Congress into this Union; but no new State shall be formed or erected within the Jurisdiction of any other State; nor any State be formed by the Junction of two or more States, or Parts of States, without the Consent of the Legislatures of the States concerned as well as of the Congress.
The Congress shall have Power to dispose of and make all needful Rules and Regulations respecting the Territory or other Property belonging to the United States; and nothing in this Constitution shall be so construed as to Prejudice any Claims of the United States, or of any particular State.

Section 3, recognized as the "property clause," concerns land the Federal Government owns and in most cases controls. Congress controlled the territory until the land was designated as a state and admitted to the Union during the western expansion. Today the Federal Government still owns up to thirty percent of the land, some in every state of the country even though the land falls within state lines. These properties include military bases, federal buildings, national parks, wildlife refuges, Indian reservations and other types of property. Over the years there's been some controversy as to why the Federal government still maintains some of this land such as Nevada where they still own and control 80%. Most recently being the Bureau of Land Management claiming the Bundy family owes about one million dollars in back fees because his cattle were eating off the government land.

Section 4
The United States shall guarantee to every State in this Union a Republican Form of Government, and shall protect each of

them against Invasion; and on Application of the Legislature, or of the Executive (when the Legislature cannot be convened), against domestic Violence.

Section 4 known as the guaranteed clause. This clause guarantees the Federal government would always:

- Operate as a republican form of government.
- Be accountable to the people—there will never be a monarchy.
- Operate under the rule of law. The federal government will protect all Americans from the enemies both foreign and domestic.

Article V

Article V of the Constitution is beginning to receive plenty of attention. This article is the tool necessary for repairing America back to her glory. The Framers wanted the Constitution to be ridged while at the same time, flexible enough to accommodate realistic change. It couldn't be so flimsy any powerful special interest group could wreak havoc on the integrity of the Constitution. They wanted flexibility for unforeseen circumstances—while keeping the integrity of the document in place thwarting any tyrannical influences. Ratifying an amendment requires the involvement and approval of many people. It requires more than a few elected leaders—and the American people will need to be involved.

Article V.

The Congress, whenever two thirds of both Houses shall deem it necessary, shall propose Amendments to this Constitution, or, on the Application of the Legislatures of two thirds of the several States, shall call a Convention for proposing Amendments, which, in either Case, shall be valid to all Intents and Purposes, as Part of this Constitution, when ratified by the Legislatures of three fourths of the several States, or by Conventions in three fourths thereof, as the one or the other Mode of Ratification may be proposed by the Congress;

Currently, there are twenty-seven amendments to the Constitution. The first ten are called the Bill of Rights. They are the original and perhaps most sacred and certainly most spoken of amendments. The Bill of Rights includes well-recognized rights such as our freedom of religion, freedoms of the press, freedom of speech and of course our right to own and bear arms or gun rights.

To add a new amendment, both houses of Congress must first pass the amendment with a two-thirds vote—not just a one-vote majority for a normal bill. Then a Convention of States is convened, and the legislature of three-fourths of the states (38 states today) must approve or ratify the amendment before adding it to the Constitution of the United States. Consequently, only twenty-seven amendments have been ratified in two hundred and thirty years. Even though there have been nearly ten thousand amendments proposed. This process prevents radical factions and special interest groups from adding a barrage of legislative rules and regulations to the document.

In chapter 17, we'll discuss how Article V will be used to repair America back to the greatness she used to be. For example, term limits on Congressmen would eliminate the career politician from Washington. That alone would benefit America simply by reducing the power of any one Congressman. It's ironic that Congress saw a need to limit the President to only two terms with the 22nd amendment in 1947 but didn't see any need to reduce their own power.

Article V allows us to bypass Congress and go directly to a convention of states and propose our own amendments. We'd need two-thirds of the states to pass a proposed amendment, and then we'd need three-quarters of the states to ratify it. That may sound like a daunting task, but to date, there are already twelve states ready to take on this challenge. If "We the People" will study and learn about the Constitution we can make a serious impact on this nation.

Provided that no Amendment which may be made prior to the Year One thousand eight hundred and eight shall in any Manner affect the first and fourth Clauses in the Ninth Section of the first Article; and that no State, without its Consent, shall be deprived of its equal Suffrage in the Senate.

Suffrage means: *A vote; a voice given in deciding a controverted question, or in the choice of a man for an office or trust.*

These two clauses in Article V were added to the document towards the end of the Constitutional Convention because of several growing concerns:

South Carolina and Georgia believed an immediate amendment might soon follow in regulating and eventually outlawing slavery. Ironically their gut feeling was correct because Alexander Hamilton, John Jay and others had already written a secret petition to abolish slavery.

Roger Sherman of Connecticut "expressed his fears that three-fourths of the States might be brought to do things fatal to particular States, as abolishing them altogether or depriving them of their equality in the Senate."

The suffrage clause allows for every state to have an equal number of votes (two votes) in the Senate regardless of the size or population of their state.

Article VI

All Debts contracted and Engagements entered into, before the Adoption of this Constitution, shall be as valid against the United States under this Constitution, as under the Confederation.

This Constitution, and the Laws of the United States which shall be made in Pursuance thereof; and all Treaties made, or which shall be made, under the Authority of the United States, shall be the supreme Law of the Land; and the Judges in every State shall be bound thereby, any Thing in the Constitution or Laws of any State to the Contrary notwithstanding.

The Senators and Representatives before mentioned, and the Members of the several State Legislatures, and all executive and judicial Officers, both of the United States and of the several States, shall be bound by Oath or Affirmation, to support this Constitution; but no religious Test shall ever be required as a Qualification to any Office or public Trust under the United States.

Before the writing and ratification of the Constitution, the thirteen states were operating under a document called the Articles of Confederation. Even though this would be a new form of government, the Founders wanted to make certain issues very clear.

The first clause states all debts and agreements the country entered prior to the Constitution are still valid and would be honored.

The second clause states we are a country of laws and all states must abide by the rules and laws written into the Constitution and any law passed by the Federal Government.

The third clause states the Senators, Representatives, and Judges are all bound by oath to support this Constitution. This is where "We the People" must step in and hold them accountable because they're not obeying this oath of office.

Finally, there'll never be a religious test required to hold office. Great Britain sponsored the Angelic Faith—unlike them, the American people didn't want a religious qualification to hold office. The intention wasn't that you couldn't let your faith show through your decisions; the Founders didn't want one faith held at a higher standard than another.

Article VII.

The Ratification of the Conventions of nine States shall be sufficient for the Establishment of this Constitution between the States so ratifying the Same.

Because there were thirteen states at the writing of this Constitution, they only needed three quarters of the thirteen states or nine states to ratify it. This one sentence—being the shortest Article, marks the replacement of the Articles of Confederation with the Constitution of the United States of America upon ratification. Note: Rhode Island was not present for the signing of the Constitution.

Done in Convention by the Unanimous Consent of the States present the Seventeenth Day of September in the Year of our Lord one thousand seven hundred and Eighty seven and of the Independence of the United States of America the Twelfth In witness whereof We have hereunto subscribed our Names,

Notice how the document is dated: *"done in Convention by the Unanimous Consent of the States present the Seventeenth Day of September in the Year of our Lord one thousand seven hundred and Eighty-seven and of the Independence of the United States of America the Twelfth."* The document is dated the 17th day of

September in the Year of our Lord, 1787 and the 12th year after the signing of our Declaration of Independence. Today, progressives have attempted to remove God and any references to Him. They try to claim the Declaration of Independence has no relationship to the Constitution. However, this closing statement shows a relationship to God and twelve years since the Declaration of Independence was signed. These documents ARE related and belong together.

G°. Washington *Presidt and deputy from Virginia*

George Washington signs as President of the Convention and thirty-nine other delegates from twelve states signed the Constitution. It's important to note the following three people were present and very instrumental in crafting the Constitution but did not sign the document: George Mason of Virginia, Edmund Randolph of Virginia and Elbridge Gerry of Massachusetts. Their reason for not signing is they believed wholeheartedly, that the Bill of Rights must go along with the Constitution to prevent tyranny. After living through all the violations of their civil rights from England, George Mason was the most outspoken person regarding not passing the Constitution without a Bill of Rights attached. Years prior, George Mason had written the Virginia Declaration of Rights.

A few notable facts regarding the signing the Constitution of the United States and the Declaration of Independence:

- The Declaration of Independence had 56 signers from 13 States
- The Constitution of the United States had 39 signers from 12 States, Rhode Island excluded
- Six people signed both documents. They were:
    - Benjamin Franklin of Pennsylvania
    - Robert Morris of Pennsylvania
    - George Clymer of Pennsylvania
    - James Wilson of Pennsylvania
    - George Read of Delaware
    - Robert Sherman of Connecticut

- Thomas Jefferson wasn't involved in the writing or signing of the Constitution because he was representing the United States in France during this time frame.
- Samuel Adams was in England representing the United States during this time frame

Chapter 15

The Bill of Rights

Originally, there were 189 proposed amendments to the Bill of Rights. After much debate, the Founders passed 12 and presented them to the states for ratification. The first amendment was never ratified at all and the second amendment was ratified just over two hundred years later on May 7, 1992, and became the twenty-seventh amendment.

The Founders struggled to get several states to ratify the Constitution because it lacked a Bill of Rights. James Madison promised they would add amendments after the Constitution became law. Being good for his word—Madison completed them, presented them to Congress, and on December 15, 1791 –ten of the amendments were ratified by the states and became law.

Congress of the United States. begun and held at the City of New York, on Wednesday the fourth of March, one thousand seven hundred and eighty nine.

THE Conventions of a number of the States, having at the time of their adopting the Constitution, expressed a desire, in order to prevent misconstruction or abuse of its powers, that further declaratory and restrictive clauses should be added: And as extending the ground of public confidence in the Government, will best ensure the beneficent ends of its institution.

RESOLVED by the Senate and House of Representatives of the United States of America, in Congress assembled, two thirds of both Houses concurring, that the following Articles be proposed to the Legislatures of the several States, as amendments to the Constitution of the United States, all, or

any of which Articles, when ratified by three fourths of the said Legislatures, to be valid to all intents and purposes, as part of the said Constitution; viz. ARTICLES in addition to, and Amendment of the Constitution of the United States of America, proposed by Congress, and ratified by the Legislatures of the several States, pursuant to the fifth Article of the original Constitution.

The Founders were committed to keeping our federal government in check and never allowing it to become a tyrannical government. They weren't satisfied with just having the enumerated powers of the new federal government specified; they wanted more protection for the liberties of the people— *"in order to prevent misconstruction or abuse of its powers, that further declaratory and restrictive clauses should be added: And as extending the ground of public confidence in the Government,"*. The public's confidence in our government being restrained was important to the Founders.

To avoid confusion, please note all twelve amendments presented to the states are outlined here. The first two did not get ratified by the states. Therefore "Article the third" became our first amendment. "Article the fourth" became the second amendment, and so on.

Article the first... After the first enumeration required by the first article of the Constitution, there shall be one Representative for every thirty thousand, until the number shall amount to one hundred, after which the proportion shall be so regulated by Congress, that there shall be not less than one hundred Representatives, nor less than one Representative for every forty thousand persons, until the number of Representatives shall amount to two hundred; after which the proportion shall be so regulated by Congress, that there shall not be less than two hundred Representatives, nor more than one Representative for every fifty thousand persons.

Again, this amendment was never ratified. If it had, the House of Representatives would have 6500 members today instead of 435. Congress passed a law in 1911 and took effect in 1913 limiting the number of House of Representatives to four hundred and thirty-five members. The Representatives are then distributed evenly by population, calculated every ten years by the census. Every state will receive at least one representative regardless of their population. Then the rest of the representatives are distributed proportionately.

Article the second... No law, varying the compensation for the services of the Senators and Representatives, shall take effect, until an election of Representatives shall have intervened.

This amendment didn't get passed until May 7, 1992, and became the twenty-seventh amendment. We'll discuss it then.

Article the third... Congress shall make no law respecting an establishment of religion, or prohibiting the free exercise thereof; or abridging the freedom of speech, or of the press; or the right of the people peaceably to assemble, and to petition the Government for a redress of grievances.
The 1st Amendment:

How can forty-five words create so much controversy? Judges, special interest groups, politician, Hollywood, and the mainstream media have all weighed in on this Amendment causing much confusion. Let's begin with the first stanza: *Congress shall make no law respecting an establishment of religion, or prohibiting the free exercise thereof;*

Looking back: in chapter 4 we learned about the faith our Founders had in God; then in chapter 6 we learned about natural laws, natural rights and the importance of electing virtuous (having high moral standards) people for office; in chapter 8 we learn how the Supreme Court ruled based on Judeo-Christian standards and the original intent of the Constitution. Additionally, in the previous chapter we learned the relationship the Constitution has with the Declaration of Independence—and the role God played in the writing of both documents.

America was dealing with a tyrannical King. If you were a Roman Catholic, you were not permitted to hold any office in England. The Anglican Church was considered the Church of England. Protestant religions such as Lutheranism, Methodist or Baptist were being planted all over Europe which the King frowned upon.

Congress shall make no law respecting an establishment of religion means the federal government cannot establish an official Church of America—or require you to be of a certain faith to run for office. The Constitution doesn't say or imply religion wasn't permitted in the public square. We've read extensively how important God and religion are to the success of the republic. Religion, (specifically, Christianity) is vital to maintaining good moral character in running a republican style government.

There's a quote in a letter Thomas Jefferson wrote to a Baptist minister stating there would be a "separation of church and state." This quote has been taken far out of context and run rapidly through our court system. The courts have sided with the Atheist religion so frequently over the past hundred years you could say they've sponsored the Atheist religion. This myth has circulated so widely you can ask people where the quote "Separation of Church and State" comes from—they'll likely say, it's part of the Constitution.

The story behind the myth begins in Europe. Many governments were outlawing protestant religions such as the Baptist religion at that time. A Baptist minister from Connecticut was concerned about rumors he was hearing—and afraid the Baptist religion would be outlawed in the states. In the letter, Jefferson was assuring the minister these rumors couldn't happen here because of our first amendment rights.

The Founders were men of faith, character and high moral standards. If the atheist interpretation of that letter were correct—Jefferson wouldn't have attended a church service two days later which was held every Sunday at the Capital Building in Washington, D.C. Also, Jefferson was the first President of the Washington D.C. school board which adopted the Holy Bible as a primary reader for the city school.

Patrick Henry said, *"The Bible is a book worth more than all other books that were ever printed."* God is the reason our country has risen to greatness. We must allow God back into our schools and public squares if we are to survive as a great nation.

Remember, according to the Declaration of Independence, all our rights come from our Creator or God. Therefore they cannot be taken away. The progressive movement wants you to believe your rights come from the government. Therefore, if the government gave you these rights than the government can take them away as well, always seek the truth.

Continuing with the first amendment: "*...or abridging the freedom of speech, or of the press;*" The amendment gives us the right to speak freely without being arrested because we disagree with the government. Controversy has grown over the years. Everything from pornography, seditious speech, artwork, and even burning of the American flag have been debated since the founding. Today free speech is being attacked and shut down if the progressives don't agree with your point of view.

The freedom of the press or media as we call it today is the only industry protected by the Constitution. The Framers understood how power corrupts people—keeping restraints on the government was vitally important. Freedom of the press is protected so the American people would always know when the government stepped out of line. Unfortunately, the media has become corrupt and agenda driven. Today, it's difficult to trust the media because they will slant their reporting to one side or the other. They will leave important and damaging stories unreported if it goes against their agenda or narrative.

One example going on today is the Trump-Russian scandal. After nearly two years of "research" and no evidence, they are still promoting it as breaking news. Yet the evidence with Hillary Clinton and Russia is overwhelming but little if any reporting on this subject. Regardless of which party you side with, if you're not a member of the 'establishment,' you can count on them destroying you in the public eye—making it difficult for men and women of good moral character to run for office. Just look at the case with Judge Roy Moore, for the Senate or Judge Brett Kavanaugh for Supreme Court Justice. Potential candidates must decide if it's worth putting their family through the challenges.

The final part of the first amendment states: "*or the right of the people peaceably to assemble, and to petition the Government for a redress of grievances.*" Americans have the right to peaceably assemble for any reason we choose without government approval. This is not the case in most socialist/communist countries. We also have the right to petition the government if we believe they're doing something illegal.

Article the fourth... A well-regulated Militia, being necessary to the security of a free State, the right of the people to keep and bear Arms, shall not be infringed.
The 2nd Amendment:

Militia means: *The body of soldiers in a state enrolled for discipline, but not engaged in actual service except in emergencies: as distinguished from regular troop, whose sole occupation is war or military service.*

What is *"A well-regulated Militia"*? Wikipedia says, "a militia generally is an army or another fighting unit that is composed of non-professional fighters, citizens of a nation or subjects of a state or government who can be called to enter a combat situation..." *"being necessary to the security of a free state."* During World War II, it's widely viewed that the Emperor of Japan said he would not attack the mainland of America because there was an American with a gun behind every blade of grass. The first thing a tyrannical dictator does is remove the guns from their citizens. This includes Hitler, Stalin, Mussolini and Castro to name a few. *"...the right of the people to keep and bear Arms, shall not be infringed,"* 'We the People' have the right to own and carry guns, and this right shall not be taken away. Remember, it's a right which comes from God. Therefore the government doesn't have the right to take it away.

The Founders wanted the people to own and maintain guns for personal protection as well as preserving liberty and freedom in case any government tries taking away our rights. You should recognize a pattern in this document. The Founders researched and studied numerous historical and current governments. In their wisdom, placed limiting restraints on this newly formed government to maintain and keep them in check.

The Federalist and the Anti-Federalist bantered over the different points in the Constitution but never disagreed with this one. They discussed whether it was enough to protect the American people but never spoke of a reason for the government to disarm the people. In Federalist Papers No. 46, James Madison wrote:

"Besides the advantage of being armed, which the Americans possess over the people of almost every other nation, the existence of subordinate governments, to which

the people are attached and by which the militia officers are appointed, forms a barrier against the enterprises of ambition, more insurmountable than any which a simple government of any form can admit of. Notwithstanding the military establishments in the several kingdoms of Europe, which are carried as far as the public resources will bear, the governments are afraid to trust the people with arms. And it is not certain that with this aid alone they would not be able to shake off their yokes."

The Founders believed it was important for people to bear arms to ensure freedom and liberty. Note the Federalist Papers were written several years before the Bill of Rights were written.

Article the fifth... No Soldier shall, in time of peace be quartered in any house, without the consent of the Owner, nor in time of war, but in a manner to be prescribed by law.
The 3rd Amendment:

Referencing the 10th, 14th, and 15th grievances' in the Declaration of Independence, notice this amendment is to protect the American people from troops taking over and living in the citizen's homes without permission. The British troops, under King George's authority, were living in the homes of the American citizens, eating their food and the citizens had no recourse. Note here; the Founders continue to refer to the Declaration of Independence as the outline or basis for the design of our Constitution.

Article the sixth... The right of the people to be secure in their persons, houses, papers, and effects, against unreasonable searches and seizures, shall not be violated, and no Warrants shall issue, but upon probable cause, supported by Oath or affirmation, and particularly describing the place to be searched, and the persons or things to be seized.
The 4th Amendment:

Watching any crime TV show, you're aware of this amendment. The Fourth Amendment through the eighth amendment deals with our rights as an American citizen from a legal/criminal standpoint. Referencing 10th grievance in the

Declaration of Independence explains why many of the Founders stressed the importance of the Bill of Rights. Both the English and the American people suffered unfair legal challenges from the King. This amendment states the police or government has no right to search or seize any of your property without a court-ordered warrant, i.e., "Let me see your search warrant."

These are important amendments that warrant your research. I recommend you take some additional time and learn why the Founders felt these critical issues are worth protecting. There's a history behind why the Founders included these in the Bill of Rights. Also, study the court challenges that exist due to these Rights.

Article the seventh... No person shall be held to answer for a capital, or otherwise infamous crime, unless on a presentment or indictment of a Grand Jury, except in cases arising in the land or naval forces, or in the Militia, when in actual service in time of War or public danger; nor shall any person be subject for the same offence to be twice put in jeopardy of life or limb; nor shall be compelled in any criminal case to be a witness against himself, nor be deprived of life, liberty, or property, without due process of law; nor shall private property be taken for public use, without just compensation.

The 5th Amendment:

"I plead the 5th". This amendment is more than just pleading our right to remain silent when being accused of an offense. It's protection against double jeopardy—being tried for the same crime more than once. It's protection against being required to testify unless we are subpoenaed by a Grand Jury. Our rights of life, liberty or property cannot be removed without a trial. We cannot have our property taken away without just compensation. This occurs when the government wants to build a highway through our property—they can build the road, but we must be compensated for it.

Article the eighth... In all criminal prosecutions, the accused shall enjoy the right to a speedy and public trial, by an impartial jury of the State and district wherein the crime shall have been committed, which district shall have been

previously ascertained by law, and to be informed of the nature and cause of the accusation; to be confronted with the witnesses against him; to have compulsory process for obtaining witnesses in his favor, and to have the Assistance of Counsel for his defense.

The 6th Amendment:

The sixth amendment speaks of our right to a speedy and public trial by an impartial jury of our peers, and in the community, the crime was committed. The defendant and the jury must be presented with the evidence against them and have the right to face their accuser. This amendment also states, "We have the right of an attorney." However, it wasn't till 1938 when the Supreme Court ruled if you can't afford one, one will be appointed to you. Prior to 1702 people weren't allowed to have anyone testify on behalf of the accused.

Article the ninth... In suits at common law, where the value in controversy shall exceed twenty dollars, the right of trial by jury shall be preserved, and no fact tried by a jury, shall be otherwise re-examined in any Court of the United States, than according to the rules of the common law.

The 7th Amendment:

This amendment gives us the right to a trial by jury. Many of the Founders did not sign the Constitution because there was not a Bill of Rights included in the original documents. This amendment was one of the main reasons the Anti-Federalist did not sign. Even Alexander Hamilton admitted in Federalist Papers No. 83 this was an oversite.

Article the tenth... Excessive bail shall not be required, nor excessive fines imposed, nor cruel and unusual punishments inflicted.

The 8th Amendment:

The eighth amendment is about charging excessive bail. But what constitutes excessive bail. The Supreme Court determined "excessive" is any amount above what would be considered enough to ensure the defendant shows up for trial. This is determined on a case-by-case basis and usually based on the character of the defendant, the crime and previous behaviors.

In England, excessive bail was used against political opponents to the King or if the King didn't want a certain person released from jail.

Article the eleventh... The enumeration in the Constitution, of certain rights, shall not be construed to deny or disparage others retained by the people.
The 9ᵗʰ Amendment:

Enumeration means: *the act of counting or telling a number, by naming each particular.*
Disparage means: *To treat with contempt; to undervalue; to lower in rank or estimation.*

The ninth amendment was added with some controversy. First, why we must have it stated in the Bill of Rights and secondly, does it perform the function it was intended to do. The Bill of Rights listed in the Constitution is not the only rights of the people. To paraphrase: Because there is a list of rights numbered one by one is not to be interpreted as these are the only rights of the people or any rights not mentioned are of any less of value.

Article the twelfth... The powers not delegated to the United States by the Constitution, nor prohibited by it to the States, are reserved to the States respectively, or to the people.
The 10ᵗʰ Amendment:

The closing Article of the Bill of Rights from our Founders acknowledges they wanted the federal government's powers limited. The people and the states are to have the power in the government. The Framers didn't want future leaders of the government taking advantage of an opportunity.

Paraphrasing—if a specific power wasn't designated to the federal government or prohibited from the states per this Constitution then the powers belong to the states or to the people—period.

The ninth and the tenth amendment were designed to close any loopholes that may pop up in the future. Again, the Founders were very careful in the wording used to assure the federal government couldn't assume certain privileges because of miss-interpretation. Our forefathers had the insight to know our modern-day leaders would take advantage of any possible loopholes. Progressives today try and convince us we are more advanced in our thinking than people of years past. People haven't changed in thousands of years, and the Founders knew it.

James Madison wrote in Federalist Papers No. 45:

> *"The powers delegated by the proposed Constitution to the federal government are few and defined. Those which are to remain in the State governments are numerous and indefinite...The powers reserved to the several States will extend to all the objects which, in the ordinary course of affairs, concern the lives, improvement, and prosperity of the State."*

ATTEST,
Frederick Augustus Muhlenberg, Speaker of the House of Representatives John Adams, Vice-President of the United States, and President of the Senate John Beckley, Clerk of the House of Representatives. Sam. A Otis Secretary of the Senate
—The four signers of the Bill of Rights with their titles.

After studying the Declaration of Independence, the Constitution of the United States and the original Bill of Rights, notice the foresight of our Founders is astounding. They truly understood too much power and authority, if unchecked would lead to corruption and tyranny. They understood tyranny was just around the corner for our country if they didn't design this Constitution properly. The reason they knew so much was simple. They were all well-read. They knew why current and historical governments rose and why they fell. They had their own previously written structure of government called the Articles of Confederation which is how they operated in the years prior to 1787. Many were lawyers and knew of the challenges England faced. The Founders were thoroughly concerned they didn't leave anything out and felt confident all bases were covered. The Founders put safeguards in place to make it difficult for us to change it—and ultimately why progressives must discredit and distort our documents. If progressives could've changed them, they would have.

After the Bill of Rights was ratified, the Founders were responsible for two more amendments (eleventh and the twelfth).

Three more if you count the twenty-seventh, ratified in 1992. In the next chapter, we will discuss the eleventh through the twenty-seventh and final amendment.

Chapter 16

Amendments 11-27

AMENDMENT XI
Passed by Congress March 4, 1794. Ratified February 7, 1795.
Note: Article III, section 2, of the Constitution was modified by amendment 11.
The Judicial power of the United States shall not be construed to extend to any suit in law or equity, commenced or prosecuted against one of the United States by Citizens of another State, or by Citizens or Subjects of any Foreign State.

Construed means: *arranged in natural order; interpreted; understood; translated*

The eleventh amendment further clarifies Article III Section II. Each state is sovereign, and the federal courts don't have the right to remove their sovereignty. The Supreme Court took on a suit where a citizen from one state sued a different state. The Supreme Court ruled in favor of the citizen. The Eleventh Amendment closes the possibility of this type of suit from happening again.

AMENDMENT XII
Passed by Congress December 9, 1803. Ratified June 15, 1804.
Note: A portion of Article II, section 1 of the Constitution was superseded by the 12th amendment.
The Electors shall meet in their respective states and vote by ballot for President and Vice-President, one of whom, at least, shall not be an inhabitant of the same state with themselves; they shall name in their ballots the person voted for as President, and in distinct ballots the person voted for as Vice-President, and they shall make distinct lists of all persons

voted for as President, and of all persons voted for as Vice-President, and of the number of votes for each, which lists they shall sign and certify, and transmit sealed to the seat of the government of the United States, directed to the President of the Senate; -- the President of the Senate shall, in the presence of the Senate and House of Representatives, open all the certificates and the votes shall then be counted; -- The person having the greatest number of votes for President, shall be the President, if such number be a majority of the whole number of Electors appointed; and if no person have such majority, then from the persons having the highest numbers not exceeding three on the list of those voted for as President, the House of Representatives shall choose immediately, by ballot, the President. But in choosing the President, the votes shall be taken by states, the representation from each state having one vote; a quorum for this purpose shall consist of a member or members from two-thirds of the states, and a majority of all the states shall be necessary to a choice. [And if the House of Representatives shall not choose a President whenever the right of choice shall devolve upon them, before the fourth day of March next following, then the Vice-President shall act as President, as in case of the death or other constitutional disability of the President. --] * The person having the greatest number of votes as Vice-President, shall be the Vice-President, if such number be a majority of the whole number of Electors appointed, and if no person have a majority, then from the two highest numbers on the list, the Senate shall choose the Vice-President; a quorum for the purpose shall consist of two-thirds of the whole number of Senators, and a majority of the whole number shall be necessary to a choice. But no person constitutionally ineligible to the office of President shall be eligible to that of Vice-President of the United States. *Superseded by section 3 of the 20th amendment.*

The twelfth amendment changed the way the president and the vice president are elected. Originally the electors had one vote each. After turning in their votes, they were tallied up, and the person that had the highest number of votes became the next president. The person with the second highest number of votes became the vice president. The twelfth amendment states that each electorate gets two votes—one vote for the president and one vote for vice president. Whoever has the highest number of votes in each category was the elected official. This was amended again with the twentieth amendment stating one vote for just the president and the president picked his running mate.

AMENDMENT XIII
Passed by Congress January 31, 1865. Ratified December 6, 1865.
Note: A portion of Article IV, section 2, of the Constitution was superseded by the 13th amendment.
Section 1
Neither slavery nor involuntary servitude, except as a punishment for crime whereof the party shall have been duly convicted, shall exist within the United States, or any place subject to their jurisdiction.
Section 2
Congress shall have power to enforce this article by appropriate legislation.

The 13th Amendment put an end to slavery after a long and brutal Civil War. Many people gave their lives for this cause—including an American President who was assassinated five days after the Civil War ended—Reference chapter 7 for more on this amendment.

Abraham Lincoln believed God was leading him every step of the way. He saw the hand of Providence working with him and the actions of the Union armies. He knew God would free the slaves and reunite the country. Lincoln just wasn't sure whether he would see it through.

In a letter to H.L. Pierce, Lincoln wrote: *"This is a world of compensation; and he who would be no slave must consent to have no slave. Those who deny freedom to others deserve it not for themselves, and under a just God, cannot long retain it."*[172]

Lincoln, in his second annual address to Congress:

---

[172] Abraham Lincoln. April 6, 1859, in a letter to H.L. Pierce and others. John Bartlett, Bartlett's Familiar Quotations (Boston: Little, Brown and Company, 1863, 1980),p. 521. Pat Robertson, America's Dates With Destiny (Nashville, TN: Thomas Nelson Publishers, 1986, p. 156

"In giving freedom to the slave, we assure freedom to the free—honorable alike in what we give and what we preserve. We shall nobly save—or meanly lose—the last, best hope of earth. Other means may succeed; this could not fail. The way is plain, peaceful, generous, just—a way which if followed the world will forever applaud and God must forever bless."[173]

Weeks before the battle at Gettysburg, Lincoln to a college president:

"I do not doubt that our country will finally come through safe and undivided. But do not misunderstand me...I do not rely on the patriotism of our people...the bravery and devotion of the boys in blud...or the loyalty and skill of our generals...But the God of our fathers, who raised up this country to be he refuge and asylum of the oppressed and downtrodden of all nations, will not let it perish now. I may not live to see it...I do not expect to see it, but God will bring us through safe."[174]

Speaking with a wounded general from Gettysburg, Lincoln said:

"When everyone seemed panic-stricken...I went to my room...and got down on my knees before Almighty God and prayed...Soon a sweet comfort crept into my soul that God Almighty had taken the whole business into His own hands..."[175]

AMENDMENT XIV
Passed by Congress June 13, 1866. Ratified July 9, 1868.
Note: Article I, section 2, of the Constitution was modified by section 2 of the 14th amendment.

---

[173] December 1, 1862, John Bartlett, Bartlett's Familiar Quotations. (Boston: Little, Brown and Company, 1863, 1980), pp. 521-524.

[174] Abraham Lincoln. June 1863, July 1-3, 1863. William J. Johnson, Abraham Lincoln, The Christian (NY: The Abington Press, 1913), pp. 109-110. Peter Marshall and David Manuel, The Glory of America (Bloomington, MN: Garborg's Heart; N Home, Inc., 1991),4.26

[175] Abraham Lincoln. July 1-3, 1863, "Lincoln's Journey in Faith" (Carmel, NY: Guideposts, February 1994), p. 36

Section 1

All persons born or naturalized in the United States, and subject to the jurisdiction thereof, are citizens of the United States and of the State wherein they reside. No State shall make or enforce any law which shall abridge the privileges or immunities of citizens of the United States; nor shall any State deprive any person of life, liberty, or property, without due process of law; nor deny to any person within its jurisdiction the equal protection of the laws.

Eight years before the ratification of the thirteenth amendment freeing slaves, a Supreme Court decision in 1857 held that blacks of African descent could not be American citizen whether free people or slaves. Three years after the thirteenth amendment, the fourteenth amendment was ratified to overrule this decision. This amendment also made clear that American citizenship trumped state citizenship—meaning a state couldn't withhold citizenship in their state preventing blacks from receiving the same privileges of that state.

Today our nation faces another challenge. It's referred to as "birthright citizenship." Illegal aliens are crossing the borders, entering the country illegally. They birth a child on American soil. It seems to be common and accepted knowledge; this child automatically becomes an American citizen. Reading the first line of the amendment: *All persons born or naturalized in the United States, and subject to the jurisdiction thereof.* This sentence states two requirements for becoming a citizen. First, you must be born or naturalized and second, you must be subject to the jurisdiction thereof. Jurisdiction thereof means you have no allegiance to another country; you have every right to be here. If the Framers of this amendment meant for "All persons born or naturalized in the United States" to be automatic citizens, they wouldn't have added "*and subject to the jurisdiction thereof.*" There wouldn't be a reason to put the statement in the amendment. Currently, there aren't any Supreme Court decisions regarding the birthrights of illegal aliens.

Section 2

Representatives shall be apportioned among the several States according to their respective numbers, counting the

whole number of persons in each State, excluding Indians not taxed. But when the right to vote at any election for the choice of electors for President and Vice-President of the United States, Representatives in Congress, the Executive and Judicial officers of a State, or the members of the Legislature thereof, is denied to any of the male inhabitants of such State, being twenty-one years of age,* and citizens of the United States, or in any way abridged, except for participation in rebellion, or other crime, the basis of representation therein shall be reduced in the proportion which the number of such male citizens shall bear to the whole number of male citizens twenty-one years of age in such State.

Article I, Section 2, Clause 3 of the Constitution states free blacks were counted as one whole person, but enslaved blacks were counted as three-fifths. This meant the state could only count three heads for every five slaves when determining the number of representatives; they were allowed for their state. Freeing all blacks gave more political power to the southern states because they received more representation in Congress. A couple of notes here. First, blacks still weren't allowed to vote until the fifteenth amendment was ratified a year and a half later. Secondly, Congress could've reduced the representation of the southern states and limited people who ran for office because they rebelled against the United States—Congress chose not to.

Section 3

No person shall be a Senator or Representative in Congress, or elector of President and Vice-President, or hold any office, civil or military, under the United States, or under any State, who, having previously taken an oath, as a member of Congress, or as an officer of the United States, or as a member of any State legislature, or as an executive or judicial officer of any State, to support the Constitution of the United States, shall have engaged in insurrection or rebellion against the same, or given aid or comfort to the enemies thereof. But Congress may by a vote of two-thirds of each House, remove such disability.

This section punishes citizens who rebel against the United States. The Confederacy rebelled with threats of seceding from the Union and their role in the Civil War. However, this became a moot point because President Andrew Johnson pardoned the crimes relating to the rebellion. Should anyone in the future be involved in any rebellion, participate in any insurrection or be part of a terrorist attack this amendment would pertain to them.

Section 4
The validity of the public debt of the United States, authorized by law, including debts incurred for payment of pensions and bounties for services in suppressing insurrection or rebellion, shall not be questioned. But neither the United States nor any State shall assume or pay any debt or obligation incurred in aid of insurrection or rebellion against the United States, or any claim for the loss or emancipation of any slave; but all such debts, obligations and claims shall be held illegal and void.

We will pay all debts incurred by the United States without question. No payments were to be made regarding the freeing of slaves. Many slave owners lost money freeing the slaves and wanted compensation from the government for the losses incurred.

Section 5
The Congress shall have the power to enforce, by appropriate legislation, the provisions of this article.
Changed by section 1 of the 26th amendment.

AMENDMENT XV
Passed by Congress February 26, 1869. Ratified February 3, 1870.
Section 1
The right of citizens of the United States to vote shall not be denied or abridged by the United States or by any State on account of race, color, or previous condition of servitude--
Section 2
The Congress shall have the power to enforce this article by appropriate legislation.

The third and last of what has become known as the Reconstruction Amendments is the right of all-American citizens to vote. This amendment allowed blacks, including the recently freed slaves the right to vote.

Abraham Lincoln knew God would free the slaves and reunite the country. He just wasn't sure if he would live to see it through. On April 15, 1865, Lincoln was assassinated 2 ½ months after the first of the three amendments passed Congress. Lincoln, being the first Republican President, was vehemently hated by the Democrats. In Dinesh D'Souza's book, Death of a Nation, he makes the statement that *"Reconstruction represented a mortal threat to a Democratic Party whose national prospects depended upon an alliance to save the slave plantation."*[176]

D'Souza makes a strong and compelling case that the Civil War was between the Republicans and the Democrats, not the North against the South as the progressives have succeeded in leading us to believe. He points out that the 13th Amendment was passed with only 16 of the 80 Democrats voting for the amendment. The 14th and the 15th amendment passed with not a single Democratic vote for these amendments.

AMENDMENT XVI
Passed by Congress July 2, 1909. Ratified February 3, 1913.
Note: Article I, section 9, of the Constitution was modified by amendment 16.
The Congress shall have power to lay and collect taxes on incomes, from whatever source derived, without apportionment among the several States, and without regard to any census or enumeration.

Apportionment means: *a dividing and assigning to each proprietor his just portion of an undivided right or property.*

It's clear this is the first amendment passed during the progressive era—the first without restrictions. Our Founders took immense pride in how the wording was expressed—keeping restraints on the federal government. They knew many years later political leaders would misinterpret the wording to meet their agenda. They expressed the importance of understanding the "original intent" of their words. The Founders designed the federal government to have just enough money and power to operate this great nation properly. Article I, Section 9 gave

---

[176] DSouza, D. (2018). *Death of a Nation.* St. Martins Press.pp.112-113

Congress the ability to raise money in the form of taxes. The criteria were difficult and perhaps a little too stringent but certainly possible. This was for good reason. With excess dollars comes excess power which the Founders tried avoiding.

One hundred years after the last amendment was written by our Founders comes the beginning of the progressive movement and its first amendment. Notice how loosely written the sixteenth amendment is. There's no limitation on what is considered income and they eliminated the guidelines of the original Constitution for accessing taxes. Paraphrasing this amendment— "Congress shall have the power to raise and collect as much taxes as they see fit from any and every source available without following any kind of guidelines what so ever." This describes our tax system today. This amendment doesn't sound anything like those written by our Founders. In fact, it goes against everything they stood for. This amendment took forty-three months to be ratified—only two amendments took longer.

Today the federal government is usurping our freedom and liberty at rates our Founders would be ashamed. Every aspect of our federal government is out of control due to power and greed. An Article V Convention would give us an opportunity to reign in our government and give power back to the people. We'll discuss this in chapter 17.

AMENDMENT XVII
Passed by Congress May 13, 1912. Ratified April 8, 1913.
Note: Article I, section 3, of the Constitution was modified by the 17th amendment.
The Senate of the United States shall be composed of two Senators from each State, elected by the people thereof, for six years; and each Senator shall have one vote. The electors in each State shall have the qualifications requisite for electors of the most numerous branch of the State legislatures.
When vacancies happen in the representation of any State in the Senate, the executive authority of such State shall issue writs of election to fill such vacancies: *Provided*, That the legislature of any State may empower the executive thereof

to make temporary appointments until the people fill the vacancies by election as the legislature may direct.

This amendment shall not be so construed as to affect the election or term of any Senator chosen before it becomes valid as part of the Constitution.

The 17th Amendment changes the way Senators are selected in America. James Madison listed five key points in Federalist Papers No. 62 & 63. Let's review these same five items and see how they compare to today. The bullet points represent today's analogy.

In the Federalist Papers No. 62 & 63, James Madison discusses five reasons for a Senate and how they are chosen.

1. The qualification of the Senators: The Senator will be more mature in age and have longer citizenship than a House of Representative. He would be more established in his behavior and morals. Madison states *"The propriety of these distinctions is explained by the nature of the senatorial trust, which, requiring greater extent of information and stability of character..."*

 ■ When most Americans vote for a Senator, age, experience, moral values and character are not top priorities. The voter's political affiliation and message take precedent in their decision making.

2. The appointment of them by the State Legislatures: The Framers designed the State Legislatures to choose the two Senators in order for the states to maintain direct influence for their agenda in Washington D.C. Madison wrote *"It is recommended by the double advantage of favoring a select appointment and of giving to the State governments such an agency in the formation of the federal government as must secure the authority of the former, and may form a convenient link between the two systems."*

 ■ This may be on a case by case basis. Prior to the 17th Amendment, the Senators had to address the issues of the state because they were selected by the state's legislature. If they wanted to be chosen again after their 6-year term they had no choice but to be directly concerned about the state issues. Today the Senators concerns seem more on a national level rather than a local level. Meaning the states have lost their priority in Congress.

3. The equality of representation in the Senate: The Framers designed the Senate to be equally represented, so one state doesn't have more influence over decision making than another state.
   ■ This may not have been affected to the extent the Senator's concern is for the states.

4. The number of Senators and the length of their terms: Madison points out in Federalist Papers No. 63 & 64 multiple reasons for having two Senators per state and staggering the appointments of these Senator with six-year terms. A republican form of government requires people of honesty and virtue. Without it, this form of government will fail. The Senate is a vital part of the overall checks and balance system the Founders put in place to help reduce the possibility of corruption. Madison continues, *"I barely remark that as the improbability of sinister combinations will be in proportion to the dissimilarity in the genius of the two bodies, it must be politic to distinguish them from each other by every circumstance which will consist with a due harmony in all proper measures and with the genuine principles of republican government."*
   ■ The Founders wanted the two Houses to be distinguishably different to reduce corruption. Now that the people vote for both the House and Senate, there are minor differences between the character of the House of Representative and the Senator because the same people are choosing both.
   ■ This may be the biggest impact. Since the Senators aren't impacted by the decisions of the state's legislature, special interest groups can influence the Senator's decisions with little repercussion from the states. This can lead to great corruption. With only 100 Senators as opposed to 435 House of Representatives, special interest groups need to influence a much smaller group of politicians to get their agenda across.

5. The Powers vested in the Senate: Among other powers, the House of Representatives have the sole power of impeachment, but the Senate has the sole power to try all Impeachments. Impeachments are for any official of the United States which Congress determines acted in any unlawful activity. The Senate will need a two-thirds majority vote to convict the official.

- There's no significant impact on this item due to the change.

Considering these five points, the biggest impact is the states lost an ally. The Founders designed the states to maintain the most control. The Senator was the special factor which allowed for the state's best interest to be represented in Washington, D.C. Instead the progressives moved more of the power to the federal government while reducing the power of the states and the people.

AMENDMENT XVIII

Passed by Congress December 18, 1917. Ratified January 16, 1919. Repealed by amendment 21.

Section 1.

After one year from the ratification of this article the manufacture, sale, or transportation of intoxicating liquors within, the importation thereof into, or the exportation thereof from the United States and all territory subject to the jurisdiction thereof for beverage purposes is hereby prohibited.

Section 2.

The Congress and the several States shall have concurrent power to enforce this article by appropriate legislation.

Section 3.

This article shall be inoperative unless it shall have been ratified as an amendment to the Constitution by the legislatures of the several States, as provided in the Constitution, within seven years from the date of the submission hereof to the States by the Congress.

Books and movies have been written about prohibition in this country. From 1920 to 1933 it was illegal to manufacture, import, transport or sell alcohol in the United States. The purpose was to control the actions of people. Fortunately, it was repealed in 1933 by the Twenty-first Amendment.

AMENDMENT XIX

Passed by Congress June 4, 1919. Ratified August 18, 1920.

The right of citizens of the United States to vote shall not be denied or abridged by the United States or by any State on account of sex.

Congress shall have power to enforce this article by appropriate legislation.

The Constitution doesn't say only men can vote, or that women could not vote. The Framers left this decision up to the states to decide, and except for New Jersey, most states limited voting to just men. There was a major women's movement that picked up a lot of steam during the early 1900s and by the time this amendment was ratified most states had already changed their voting policy to allow women to vote.

AMENDMENT XX

Passed by Congress March 2, 1932. Ratified January 23, 1933.

Note: Article I, section 4, of the Constitution was modified by section 2 of this amendment. In addition, a portion of the 12th amendment was superseded by section 3.

Section 1.

The terms of the President and the Vice President shall end at noon on the 20th day of January, and the terms of Senators and Representatives at noon on the 3d day of January, of the years in which such terms would have ended if this article had not been ratified; and the terms of their successors shall then begin.

Section 2.

The Congress shall assemble at least once in every year, and such meeting shall begin at noon on the 3d day of January, unless they shall by law appoint a different day.

Section 3.

If, at the time fixed for the beginning of the term of the President, the President elect shall have died, the Vice President elect shall become President. If a President shall not have been chosen before the time fixed for the beginning

of his term, or if the President elect shall have failed to qualify, then the Vice President elect shall act as President until a President shall have qualified; and the Congress may by law provide for the case wherein neither a President elect nor a Vice President elect shall have qualified, declaring who shall then act as President, or the manner in which one who is to act shall be selected, and such person shall act accordingly until a President or Vice President shall have qualified.

Section 4.

The Congress may by law provide for the case of the death of any of the persons from whom the House of Representatives may choose a President whenever the right of choice shall have devolved upon them, and for the case of the death of any of the persons from whom the Senate may choose a Vice President whenever the right of choice shall have devolved upon them.

Section 5.

Sections 1 and 2 shall take effect on the 15th day of October following the ratification of this article.

Section 6.

This article shall be inoperative unless it shall have been ratified as an amendment to the Constitution by the legislatures of three-fourths of the several States within seven years from the date of its submission.

This amendment made fundamental and procedural changes to the Constitution. Worth noting is the shortening of the lame-duck session of Congress in Section 1—the time between the new Congress and the new President taking office.

AMENDMENT XXI

Passed by Congress February 20, 1933. Ratified December 5, 1933.

Section 1.

The eighteenth article of amendment to the Constitution of the United States is hereby repealed.

Section 2.

The transportation or importation into any State, Territory, or possession of the United States for delivery or use therein of intoxicating liquors, in violation of the laws thereof, is hereby prohibited.

Section 3.

This article shall be inoperative unless it shall have been ratified as an amendment to the Constitution by conventions in the several States, as provided in the Constitution, within seven years from the date of the submission hereof to the States by the Congress.

This represents the repeal of the 18th amendment—giving the states back the right to manufacture, distribute and regulate alcohol without federal government interference.

AMENDMENT XXII

Passed by Congress March 21, 1947. Ratified February 27, 1951.

Section 1.

No person shall be elected to the office of the President more than twice, and no person who has held the office of President, or acted as President, for more than two years of a term to which some other person was elected President shall be elected to the office of the President more than once. But this Article shall not apply to any person holding the office of President when this Article was proposed by the Congress, and shall not prevent any person who may be holding the office of President, or acting as President, during the term within which this Article becomes operative from holding the office of President or acting as President during the remainder of such term.

Section 2.

This article shall be inoperative unless it shall have been ratified as an amendment to the Constitution by the legislatures of three-fourths of the several States within seven years from the date of its submission to the States by the Congress.

This amendment set term limits on the President of the United States to a maximum of two terms. Franklin D. Roosevelt finished four terms as President, so Congress decided to pass this amendment. The Founders had mixed opinion on term limits for the president but ultimately decided against it. Its interesting

Congress felt the need for term limits on the president but not for themselves. They limited the president to two-term but saw no need to limit their terms. This is a notable example of how power corrupts. The President plays no part in amendments, but Congress does. Perhaps if the President had to sign the amendment, he might have required Congress to put term limits on themselves as well.

AMENDMENT XXIII
Passed by Congress June 16, 1960. Ratified March 29, 1961.
Section1
The District constituting the seat of Government of the United States shall appoint in such manner as the Congress may direct:
A number of electors of President and Vice President equal to the whole number of Senators and Representatives in Congress to which the District would be entitled if it were a State, but in no event more than the least populous State; they shall be in addition to those appointed by the States, but they shall be considered, for the purposes of the election of President and Vice President, to be electors appointed by a State; and they shall meet in the District and perform such duties as provided by the twelfth article of amendment.
Section2
The Congress shall have power to enforce this article by appropriate legislation.

The passing of this amendment gave citizens living in the ten-mile by ten-mile square land we call Washington D.C. the right to vote for the President. Because they're not considered a state these rights hadn't been granted the district. The twenty-third amendment gave them the right to vote for president. They still don't have any Congressional representation.

AMENDMENT XXIV
Passed by Congress August 27, 1962. Ratified January 23, 1964.
Section 1.
The right of citizens of the United States to vote in any primary or other election for President or Vice President, for electors for President or Vice President, or for Senator or

Representative in Congress, shall not be denied or abridged by the United States or any State by reason of failure to pay any poll tax or other tax.
Section 2.
The Congress shall have power to enforce this article by appropriate legislation.

A poll tax is a flat uniform tax applied to every citizen base on the census. This tax has been utilized by governments as income for centuries. The United States enacted the poll tax, mostly in the southern states, for keeping many black and poor white citizens from voting. If a person hadn't paid their poll tax by a certain date, they were ineligible to vote in the upcoming election.   Congress stopped this with the twenty-fourth amendment.

AMENDMENT XXV
Passed by Congress July 6, 1965. Ratified February 10, 1967.
Note: Article II, section 1, of the Constitution was affected by the 25th amendment.
Section 1.
In case of the removal of the President from office or of his death or resignation, the Vice President shall become President.
Section 2.
Whenever there is a vacancy in the office of the Vice President, the President shall nominate a Vice President who shall take office upon confirmation by a majority vote of both Houses of Congress.
Section 3.
Whenever the President transmits to the President pro tempore of the Senate and the Speaker of the House of Representatives his written declaration that he is unable to discharge the powers and duties of his office, and until he transmits to them a written declaration to the contrary, such powers and duties shall be discharged by the Vice President as Acting President.
Section 4.
Whenever the Vice President and a majority of either the principal officers of the executive departments or of such

other body as Congress may by law provide, transmit to the President pro tempore of the Senate and the Speaker of the House of Representatives their written declaration that the President is unable to discharge the powers and duties of his office, the Vice President shall immediately assume the powers and duties of the office as Acting President.

Thereafter, when the President transmits to the President pro tempore of the Senate and the Speaker of the House of Representatives his written declaration that no inability exists, he shall resume the powers and duties of his office unless the Vice President and a majority of either the principal officers of the executive department or of such other body as Congress may by law provide, transmit within four days to the President pro tempore of the Senate and the Speaker of the House of Representatives their written declaration that the President is unable to discharge the powers and duties of his office. Thereupon Congress shall decide the issue, assembling within forty-eight hours for that purpose if not in session. If the Congress, within twenty-one days after receipt of the latter written declaration, or, if Congress is not in session, within twenty-one days after Congress is required to assemble, determines by two-thirds vote of both Houses that the President is unable to discharge the powers and duties of his office, the Vice President shall continue to discharge the same as Acting President; otherwise, the President shall resume the powers and duties of his office.

Pro tempore: *temporary; for the time being; Note*—not in N. Webster's 1828 dictionary

The twenty-fifth amendment completely clarifies the process for removing a sitting President in the event he's unfit to perform the duties of the office of President—and make clear who shall replace the President. Throughout American history, several Vice Presidents have taken over as President, and in each case, questions arose whether he's the acting President or actual President.

Three ways to remove a sitting President:
- The President himself can notify the Vice President (President of the Senate) and the Speaker of the House of his inability to temporarily or permanently be removed.
- The Vice President with a majority of the President's executive officers can present a case to Congress to have the President removed.
- The Vice President with a majority of the body of Congress.

AMENDMENT XXVI
Passed by Congress March 23, 1971. Ratified July 1, 1971.
Note: Amendment 14, section 2, of the Constitution was modified by section 1 of the 26th amendment.
Section 1.
The right of citizens of the United States, who are eighteen years of age or older, to vote shall not be denied or abridged by the United States or by any State on account of age.
Section 2.
The Congress shall have power to enforce this article by appropriate legislation.

The 26th Amendment allows 18-year-old citizens the opportunity to participate in the election process—to vote.

AMENDMENT XXVII
Originally proposed Sept. 25, 1789. Ratified May 7, 1992.
No law, varying the compensation for the services of the Senators and Representatives, shall take effect, until an election of Representatives shall have intervened.

This amendment was part of the original twelve Bill of Rights. This amendment states when Congress passes a bill raising their salary, the new salary cannot take effect until the beginning of their next term of office. This forces Congressmen to face the electorate over this compensation increase before receiving any monetary gain. This amendment has become a moot point because in 1989 Congress passed a bill authorizing automatic pay increases each year instead of facing their constituents every-time they give themselves a raise.

This concludes the study of our Constitution. America has drifted so far out of kilter; it's going to take miracles from God to restore us to greatness. There is a lot of good people, both young and old, in this nation that are willing to do the heavy lifting to revive this great experiment our Founders gave their lives, fortunes and sacred honor for. However, we must start with a return to the foundation: God first and our Constitution second.

It's imperative for us all to continue reading, studying, researching and sharing what we've learned. We must seek God's face and pray for a spiritual revival. On October 11, 1798, in speaking to the military, President John Adams said:

> *"We have no government armed with power capable of contending with human passions unbridled by morality and religion. Avarice, ambition, revenge, or gallantry, would break the strongest cords of our Constitution as a whale goes through a net. Our Constitution was made only for a moral and religious people. It is wholly inadequate to the government of any other."*[177]

If "We the People" hold our leaders accountable for everything they do, we'll change the pattern of chaos—and the freedom and liberty our Founders fought and died for will not be in vain. Trusting our political leaders without verifying the truth will prove destructive for America.

Become a truth seeker…

---

[177] Adams, John. (Oct.11, 1798), Letter to the Massachusetts Militia

Chapter 17

Secrets Applied Restores America

So how in God's green earth do we repair this Great Nation? A better question might be: can this nation be repaired? In a letter to Thomas Jefferson from John Adams, John writes: *Have you ever found in history, one single example of a Nation thoroughly corrupted that was afterward restored to virtue?* Would our Founders recognize the government we have today? When the Constitution of the United States was finished, Ben Franklin was asked: What kind of government did you give us? He answered, *"a republic if you can keep it."*

Crime of all forms are at an ever-increasing rate. The pornography industry makes billions of dollars per year. The divorce rate is at an all-time high and continuing to rise. Families are becoming extinct—children are being raised by single moms or dads. Illegal immigration is spinning out of control. Corruption in our political and business sectors is indescribable. The mainstream media has aligned itself with the corruption in Washington and can't be trusted. Churches are struggling to survive—and have become stale and irrelevant. Pastors are afraid to speak the truth of the Word of God. People are lost, confused and don't know who to follow—and in many cases, don't care.

The progressive movement has divided us every way possible. They've pitted the rich against the poor—young against the old—blacks against the whites—Christians against everyone else. Republicans against the Democrats—liberals against conservatives—union loyalist against non-union loyalist, anyway they can divide us they have. And the more divided this nation, the easier it is to control the agenda—and consequently controlling... "We the People."

We ask ourselves—what can I do? Or—there's nothing I can do about what's going on in Washington. I vote, or I don't vote, or I don't see what difference it makes for me to vote—politicians do what they want anyway.

This all plays into the hands of the political elite. We are people who've given up. We have been made to believe our only hope is in the almighty politicians. Our schools are virtually indoctrination chambers for the government. Our newspapers and news media outlets are primarily propaganda machines for the ruling class. The court systems are making decisions based on their political views instead of following the original intent of the Constitution...Our government bureaucratic agencies are making laws that affect our daily lives instead of our elected Congressmen and women. On top of that, our Congressmen are maintaining a blind eye instead of using their Constitutional power to stop them. They've become complicit and have little concern for the people who elected them.

So today, when you ask: "what difference does my vote make anyway?" I can tell you it probably doesn't make much difference at all. And that's our fault. You see, just voting is all the political elite want you to do. They know most people won't get involved but try to live their lives according to the laws that govern them. We've become no more than paid slaves to the king and his court, or should I say to the President and his Congressman and Judges.

Getting back to the original question at the start. How do we repair this nation? America was designed to be a melting pot for all people to be free. Do you need to be a Christian to live here or convert to Christianity for us to fix this nation? No. If you are Jewish, Muslim, Buddhist, Atheist or no religion at all, you can live in America and still participate in the repairing of this nation. America was created for religious freedom; therefore, to say you must be a Christian to live here and prosper would be against everything the Founders had intended.

We spent a whole chapter on describing who our Founders were and how many of them were strong believers in the God of the universe and His Son Jesus. We learned the importance of being a virtuous people—with a high moral character and integrity. This sets the foundation for a powerful structure to be created. In other words, you don't need to be of the same faith, but you must follow the Godly principles that He set. We can fly a plane because the designer understood the principles of gravity even though they never saw gravity. We can grow a garden because we understand the principles of planting seeds and watering them. We can fix this nation if we follow the principles that created it. Progressivism took close to one hundred and twenty years to strip this nation of her foundation. It may take that long to fix it--but we must start now.

So where do we begin? Let's start with you. Since you're almost done reading this book, let me ask you several questions. What have you learned from the reading? Do you have a good grasp on the Constitution? Do you understand why the Constitution was written to limit the federal government and give the bulk of the power to the states? Can you see how that gives "We the People" more control? Have you noticed how our government has ignored our founding documents?

How about the stories? Why haven't you ever heard most if not all the stories from chapter 4 in the past? Why has that been hidden from us? One hundred and twenty years ago the Bible and the Constitution was taught in schools—and the people knew the answers to these questions which explains why the progressive movement couldn't gain any ground. The elite of the day figured they needed to do three things. Remove God from the schools, minimize the value of the Constitution and discredit the Founding Fathers. Since doing all three of these, the progressive movement has taken control of this country, and consequently, we're left with the issues described earlier.

To repair this nation, you must first have the answers to these questions. I trust you've learned a great deal but please don't just take my word as gospel but seek the truth for yourself. There's so much more detailed information not covered here which is important for you to discover. The Founders felt it was important for you to "know and study" the Constitution. Make this book the beginning of your journey.

Since we now know what the progressive movement has done to change our nation into a divided, corrupted and misguided country. It stands to reason; all we need to do is reverse the direction to say an 'anti-progressive' movement. Let's start by allowing God back into our schools. Let's study and understand the Declaration of Independence and our Constitution. Finally, let's teach everyone who the Founders really were. Let's share the miracles that took place during the Revolutionary War. Let's develop our faith and seek God's wisdom so we can overcome some incredibly challenging times ahead. Let's restore America to greatness.

There's never been a country in the history of the world that has been corrupted like we are and been able to restore itself to a virtuous nation (Adams and Jefferson). Does that mean there's no hope for us? I for one believe God's not done with America yet. There are still too many people who don't know Jesus. Therefore, I believe God would be willing to restore America to greatness.

> *"If my people, who are called by my name, will humble themselves and pray and seek my face and turn from their wicked ways, then I will hear from heaven, and I will forgive their sin and will heal their land"* (2 Chronicles 7:14 NIV).

This scripture alone says everything we need to do to fix this nation. Jesus said in Matthew 18:20NIV *"For where two or three gathers in my name, there am I with them."* In John 14:13NIV Jesus said, *"And I will do whatever you ask in my name, so that the Father may be glorified in the Son."*

So, to repair America, we must First, pray as a nation. I have a vision of using social media such as Slack or some type of website, App or Twitter account we can all unite around and pray for the sole purpose of God's intervention into the healing of this nation. If "We the People" come together for that common purpose alone, we can make an impact on America which by-itself would be a powerful start.

Second; we must allow God back into the schools. Many horrible incidents have happened in our schools over the last several years. Could this be happening because we have kicked God out? Let's ask Him back in. Don't believe the lies that say, God is not allowed in the schools or the public square. It's ironic and sickening that prison officials are begging for missionaries to bring God to the people in the cells, but schools have kicked God out. After studying the Constitution, you know it doesn't say we must keep God out. The Constitution is a document which tells us what the government CAN'T do. It can't establish a religion or take away our guns. It can't quarter soldiers in our homes or search our home without a warrant. It never says what The People can't do. **It only states what the government CAN'T do.** If we choose to teach our children about God in school—it's our decision, not the governments. If we choose to have a nativity scene in the public square—it's our decision, not the governments. The government wasn't given the power to tell "We the People" what we can and can't do. The government doesn't have that authority.

The third thing we must do to repair America is to continue our study of the Constitution of the United States. The Founders believe every classroom should have a copy of the Constitution and the Holy Bible. The more you know, the better. This book is just for starters to whet your appetite. There are free online courses you can take from Hillsdale College that will help you tremendously.

Next, read more about the Founders and the founding of America. However, I caution you; the progressive movement has produced books designed to smear the Founders and promote their agenda. Research the author and see if there's some sort of hidden agenda in their writings. Unfortunately, the world has become so corrupt; it's hard to decipher the truth which is another reason to seek God's face in all you do. He is the one standard we can trust.

Finally, we must act. There's a movement called the Convention of States Project led by a man named Mark Meckler and promoted by Mark Levin and others. The Founders knew "We the People" could be misled and become lackadaisical. They knew when power is granted to people it will never be enough and they will continue to want more. They knew the federal government would more than likely become way too powerful and usurp the power from the people. So, in Article V of the Constitution, they added a way for the people to regain control of Washington. This movement is growing rapidly, and we all need to get behind it. This is a well-organized group of grassroots Americans who are committed to establishing a successful Convention of States as outlined in Article V of the Constitution. This movement has spread across the whole country and is getting noticed. Mark Levin has a book out called The Liberty Amendments. It discusses many important amendments we can add to our Constitution to take back America. It talks about getting behind the Convention of States movement and how this will help in restoring virtue back to America.

The goals of this grass-roots operation are to call a Convention of States to limit the power and jurisdiction of the federal government, impose term limits and fiscally restrain our elected officials.

Every state is divided into a certain number of districts. We're looking for a district captain plus 100 volunteers in at least 75% of the 5000 plus districts in America. Currently, we are growing strong with over 3 million people involved and looking to increase to 10 million. Go to www.cosaction.com/strategy to learn more and sign up to volunteer as freedom fighters. Our children and grandchildren are counting on us.

So, to conclude, seek God first. The Founders claimed there's never been a country come back from a corrupt nation and become virtuous. I might add there have never been a People who have the spirit of "American Exceptionalism" built in them. Our military, our businesses, our foundation has all been wrapped in the spirit of Greatness. We have made many mistakes but have been able to rebound from them and grow. We've met many challenges and overcome them. There's no reason for us to stop believing in America now.

Our problems today are numerous and overwhelming. These challenges are both internal and external. They cannot and will not be corrected by the power of any one man or women. We need a power that's willing and able to fix the hearts of man. A power that's willing to right the wrongs which the evil one has injected into this nation. We need The Power that created American Exceptionalism in the hearts of all Americans. We need the God of our Founders. We need the God that created the Heavens and the Earth and each one of us. And without His intervention, there is no hope. Seek God's help by getting on your knees and praying every day for Him to intercede in the affairs of man. Then, and only then will we see America restored to Greatness. May God continue to bless you and the United States of America.

Appendix A

The Declaration of Independence: A Transcription

IN CONGRESS, July 4, 1776.

The unanimous Declaration of the thirteen united States of America,

When in the Course of human events, it becomes necessary for one people to dissolve the political bands which have connected them with another, and to assume among the powers of the earth, the separate and equal station to which the Laws of Nature and of Nature's God entitle them, a decent respect to the opinions of mankind requires that they should declare the causes which impel them to the separation.

We hold these truths to be self-evident, that all men are created equal, that they are endowed by their Creator with certain unalienable Rights, that among these are Life, Liberty and the pursuit of Happiness.--That to secure these rights, Governments are instituted among Men, deriving their just powers from the consent of the governed, --That whenever any Form of Government becomes destructive of these ends, it is the Right of the People to alter or to abolish it, and to institute new Government, laying its foundation on such principles and organizing its powers in such form, as to them shall seem most likely to affect their Safety and Happiness. Prudence, indeed, will dictate that Governments long established should not be changed for light and transient causes; and accordingly all experience hath shewn, that mankind are more disposed to suffer, while evils are sufferable, than to right themselves by abolishing the forms to which they are accustomed. But when a long train of abuses and usurpations, pursuing invariably the same Object evinces a design to reduce them under absolute Despotism, it is their right, it is their duty, to throw off such Government, and to provide new Guards for their future security.--Such has been the patient sufferance of these Colonies; and such is now the necessity which constrains them to alter their former Systems of Government. The history of the present King of Great Britain is a history of repeated injuries and usurpations, all having in direct object the establishment of an absolute Tyranny over these States. To prove this, let Facts be submitted to a candid world.

He has refused his Assent to Laws, the most wholesome and necessary for the public good.

He has forbidden his Governors to pass Laws of immediate and pressing importance, unless suspended in their operation till his Assent should be obtained; and when so suspended, he has utterly neglected to attend to them.

He has refused to pass other Laws for the accommodation of large districts of people, unless those people would relinquish the right of Representation in the Legislature, a right inestimable to them and formidable to tyrants only.

He has called together legislative bodies at places unusual, uncomfortable, and distant from the depository of their public Records, for the sole purpose of fatiguing them into compliance with his measures.

He has dissolved Representative Houses repeatedly, for opposing with manly firmness his invasions on the rights of the people.

He has refused for a long time, after such dissolutions, to cause others to be elected; whereby the Legislative powers, incapable of Annihilation, have returned to the People at large for their exercise; the State remaining in the meantime exposed to all the dangers of invasion from without, and convulsions within.

He has endeavored to prevent the population of these States; for that purpose obstructing the Laws for Naturalization of Foreigners; refusing to pass others to encourage their migrations hither, and raising the conditions of new Appropriations of Lands.

He has obstructed the Administration of Justice, by refusing his Assent to Laws for establishing Judiciary powers.

He has made Judges dependent on his Will alone, for the tenure of their offices, and the amount and payment of their salaries.

He has erected a multitude of New Offices, and sent hither swarms of Officers to harass our people, and eat out their substance.

He has kept among us, in times of peace, Standing Armies without the Consent of our legislatures.

He has affected to render the Military independent of and superior to the Civil power.

He has combined with others to subject us to a jurisdiction foreign to our constitution, and unacknowledged by our laws; giving his Assent to their Acts of pretended Legislation:

For Quartering large bodies of armed troops among us:

For protecting them, by a mock Trial, from punishment for any Murders which they should commit on the Inhabitants of these States:

For cutting off our Trade with all parts of the world:

For imposing Taxes on us without our Consent:

For depriving us in many cases, of the benefits of Trial by Jury:

For transporting us beyond Seas to be tried for pretended offences

For abolishing the free System of English Laws in a neighboring Province, establishing therein an Arbitrary government, and enlarging its Boundaries so as to render it at once an example and fit instrument for introducing the same absolute rule into these Colonies:

For taking away our Charters, abolishing our most valuable Laws, and altering fundamentally the Forms of our Governments:

For suspending our own Legislatures, and declaring themselves invested with power to legislate for us in all cases whatsoever.

He has abdicated Government here, by declaring us out of his Protection and waging War against us.

He has plundered our seas, ravaged our Coasts, burnt our towns, and destroyed the lives of our people.

He is at this time transporting large Armies of foreign Mercenaries to complete the works of death, desolation and tyranny, already begun with circumstances of Cruelty & perfidy scarcely paralleled in the most barbarous ages, and totally unworthy the Head of a civilized nation.

He has constrained our fellow Citizens taken Captive on the high Seas to bear Arms against their Country, to become the executioners of their friends and Brethren, or to fall themselves by their Hands.

He has excited domestic insurrections amongst us, and has endeavored to bring on the inhabitants of our frontiers, the merciless Indian Savages, whose known rule of warfare is an undistinguished destruction of all ages, sexes and conditions.

In every stage of these Oppressions We have petitioned for Redress in the most humble terms: Our repeated Petitions have been answered only by repeated injury. A Prince whose character is thus marked by every act which may define a Tyrant, is unfit to be the ruler of a free people.

Nor have We been wanting in attentions to our British brethren. We have warned them from time to time of attempts by their legislature to extend an unwarrantable jurisdiction over us. We have reminded them of the circumstances of our emigration and settlement here. We have appealed to their native justice and magnanimity, and we have conjured them by the ties of our common kindred to disavow these usurpations, which, would inevitably interrupt our connections and correspondence. They too have been deaf to the voice of justice and of consanguinity. We must, therefore, acquiesce in the necessity, which denounces our Separation, and hold them, as we hold the rest of mankind, Enemies in War, in Peace Friends.

We, therefore, the Representatives of the united States of America, in General Congress, Assembled, appealing to the Supreme Judge of the world for the rectitude of our intentions, do, in the Name, and by Authority of the good People of these Colonies, solemnly publish and declare, That these United Colonies are, and of Right ought to be Free and Independent States; that they are Absolved from all Allegiance to the British Crown, and that all political connection between them and the State of Great Britain, is and ought to be totally dissolved; and that as Free and Independent States, they have full Power to levy War, conclude Peace, contract Alliances, establish Commerce, and to do all other Acts and Things which Independent States may of right do. And for the support of this Declaration, with a firm reliance on the protection of divine Providence, we mutually pledge to each other our Lives, our Fortunes and our sacred Honor.

Delaware:	Rhode Island:	South Carolina:
George Reed	Stephen Hopkins	Edward Rutledge
Caesar Rodney	William Ellery	Arthur Middleton
Thomas McKean	New York:	Thomas Lynch, Jr.
Pennsylvania:	Lewis Morris	Thomas Heyward, Jr.
George Clymer	Philip Livingston	New Jersey:
Benjamin Franklin	Francis Lewis	Abraham Clark
Robert Morris	William Floyd	John Hart
John Morton	Georgia:	Francis Hopkinson

Benjamin Rush
George ross
James Smith
James Wilson
George Taylor
Massachusetts:
John Adams
Samuel Adams
John Hancock
Robert Treat Paine
Elbridge Gerry
New Hampshire:
Josiah Bartlett
William Whipple
Matthew Thornton

Button Gwinnett
Lyman Hall
George Walton
Virginia:
Richard Henry Lee
Francis Lightfoot Lee
Carter Braxton
Benjamin Harrison
Thomas Jefferson
George Wythe
Thomas Nelson, Jr.
North Carolina:
William Hooper
John Penn
Joseph Hewes

Richard Stockton
John Witherspoon
Connecticut:
Samuel Huntington
Roger Sherman
William Williams
Oliver Wolcott
Maryland:
Charles Carroll
Samuel Chase
Thomas Stone
William Paca

Appendix B

The Constitution of the United States: A Transcription[9]

We the People of the United States, in Order to form a more perfect Union, establish Justice, insure domestic Tranquility, provide for the common defense, promote the general Welfare, and secure the Blessings of Liberty to ourselves and our Posterity, do ordain and establish this Constitution for the United States of America.

Article I.

Section 1

All legislative Powers herein granted shall be vested in a Congress of the United States, which shall consist of a Senate and House of Representatives.

Section 2

The House of Representatives shall be composed of Members chosen every second Year by the People of the several States, and the Electors in each State shall have the Qualifications requisite for Electors of the most numerous Branch of the State Legislature.

No Person shall be a Representative who shall not have attained to the Age of twenty-five Years, and been seven Years a Citizen of the United States, and who shall not, when elected, be an Inhabitant of that State in which he shall be chosen.

Representatives and direct Taxes shall be apportioned among the several States which may be included within this Union, according to their respective Numbers, which shall be determined by adding to the whole Number of free Persons, including those bound to Service for a Term of Years, and excluding Indians not taxed, three fifths of all other Persons. The actual Enumeration shall be made within three Years after the first Meeting of the Congress of the United States, and within every subsequent Term of ten Years, in such Manner as they shall by Law direct. The Number of Representatives shall not exceed one for every thirty Thousand, but each State shall have at Least one Representative; and until such enumeration shall be made, the State of New Hampshire shall be entitled to choose three, Massachusetts eight, Rhode-Island and Providence Plantations one, Connecticut five, New-York six, New Jersey four, Pennsylvania eight, Delaware one, Maryland six, Virginia ten, North Carolina five, South Carolina five, and Georgia three.

When vacancies happen in the Representation from any State, the Executive Authority thereof shall issue Writs of Election to fill such Vacancies.

The House of Representatives shall choose their Speaker and other Officers; and shall have the sole Power of Impeachment.

Section 3

The Senate of the United States shall be composed of two Senators from each State, chosen by the Legislature thereof, for six Years; and each Senator shall have one Vote.

Immediately after they shall be assembled in Consequence of the first Election, they shall be divided as equally as may be into three Classes. The Seats of the Senators of the first Class shall be vacated at the Expiration of the second Year, of the second Class at the Expiration of the fourth Year, and of the third Class at the Expiration of the sixth Year, so that one third may be chosen every second Year; and if Vacancies happen by Resignation, or otherwise, during the Recess of the Legislature of any State, the Executive thereof may make temporary Appointments until the next Meeting of the Legislature, which shall then fill such Vacancies.

No Person shall be a Senator who shall not have attained to the Age of thirty Years, and been nine Years a Citizen of the United States, and who shall not, when elected, be an Inhabitant of that State for which he shall be chosen.

The Vice President of the United States shall be President of the Senate, but shall have no Vote, unless they be equally divided.

The Senate shall choose their other Officers, and also a President pro tempore, in the Absence of the Vice President, or when he shall exercise the Office of President of the United States.

The Senate shall have the sole Power to try all Impeachments. When sitting for that Purpose, they shall be on Oath or Affirmation. When the President of the United States is tried, the Chief Justice shall preside: And no Person shall be convicted without the Concurrence of two thirds of the Members present.

Judgment in Cases of Impeachment shall not extend further than to removal from Office, and disqualification to hold and enjoy any Office of honor, Trust or Profit under the United States: but the Party convicted shall nevertheless be liable and subject to Indictment, Trial, Judgment and Punishment, according to Law.

Section 4

The Times, Places and Manner of holding Elections for Senators and Representatives, shall be prescribed in each State by the Legislature thereof; but the Congress may at any time by Law make or alter such Regulations, except as to the Places of choosing Senators.

The Congress shall assemble at least once in every Year, and such Meeting shall be on the first Monday in December, unless they shall by Law appoint a different Day.

Section 5

Each House shall be the Judge of the Elections, Returns and Qualifications of its own Members, and a Majority of each shall constitute a Quorum to do Business; but a smaller Number may adjourn from day to day, and may be authorized to compel the Attendance of absent Members, in such Manner, and under such Penalties as each House may provide.

Each House may determine the Rules of its Proceedings, punish its Members for disorderly Behavior, and, with the Concurrence of two thirds, expel a Member.

Each House shall keep a Journal of its Proceedings, and from time to time publish the same, excepting such Parts as may in their Judgment require Secrecy; and the Yeas and Nays of the Members of either House on any question shall, at the Desire of one fifth of those Present, be entered on the Journal.

Neither House, during the Session of Congress, shall, without the Consent of the other, adjourn for more than three days, nor to any other Place than that in which the two Houses shall be sitting.

Section 6

The Senators and Representatives shall receive a Compensation for their Services, to be ascertained by Law, and paid out of the Treasury of the United States. They shall in all Cases, except Treason, Felony and Breach of the Peace, be privileged from Arrest during their Attendance at the Session of their respective Houses, and in going to and returning from the same; and for any Speech or Debate in either House, they shall not be questioned in any other Place.

No Senator or Representative shall, during the Time for which he was elected, be appointed to any civil Office under the Authority of the United States, which shall have been created, or the Emoluments whereof shall have been increased during such time; and no Person holding any Office under the United States, shall be a Member of either House during his Continuance in Office.

Section 7

All Bills for raising Revenue shall originate in the House of Representatives; but the Senate may propose or concur with Amendments as on other Bills.

Every Bill which shall have passed the House of Representatives and the Senate, shall, before it become a Law, be presented to the President of the United States; If he approve he shall sign it, but if not he shall return it, with his Objections to that House in which it shall have originated, who shall enter the Objections at large on their Journal, and proceed to reconsider it. If after such Reconsideration two thirds of that House shall agree to pass the Bill, it shall be sent, together with the Objections, to the other House, by which it shall likewise be reconsidered, and if approved by two thirds of that House, it shall become a Law. But in all such Cases the Votes of both Houses shall be determined by yeas and Nays, and the Names of the Persons voting for and against the Bill shall be entered on the Journal of each House respectively. If any Bill shall not be returned by the President within ten Days (Sundays excepted) after it shall have been presented to him, the Same shall be a Law, in like Manner as if he had signed it, unless the Congress by their Adjournment prevent its Return, in which Case it shall not be a Law.

Every Order, Resolution, or Vote to which the Concurrence of the Senate and House of Representatives may be necessary (except on a question of Adjournment) shall be presented to the President of the United States; and before the Same shall take Effect, shall be approved by him, or being disapproved by him, shall be repassed by two thirds of the Senate and House of Representatives, according to the Rules and Limitations prescribed in the Case of a Bill.

Section 8

The Congress shall have Power To lay and collect Taxes, Duties, Imposts and Excises, to pay the Debts and provide for the common Defense and general Welfare of the United States; but all Duties, Imposts and Excises shall be uniform throughout the United States;

To borrow Money on the credit of the United States;

To regulate Commerce with foreign Nations, and among the several States, and with the Indian Tribes;

To establish an uniform Rule of Naturalization, and uniform Laws on the subject of Bankruptcies throughout the United States;

To coin Money, regulate the Value thereof, and of foreign Coin, and fix the Standard of Weights and Measures;

To provide for the Punishment of counterfeiting the Securities and current Coin of the United States;

To establish Post Offices and post Roads;

To promote the Progress of Science and useful Arts, by securing for limited Times to Authors and Inventors the exclusive Right to their respective Writings and Discoveries;

To constitute Tribunals inferior to the Supreme Court;

To define and punish Piracies and Felonies committed on the high Seas, and Offences against the Law of Nations;

To declare War, grant Letters of Marque and Reprisal, and make Rules concerning Captures on Land and Water;

To raise and support Armies, but no Appropriation of Money to that Use shall be for a longer Term than two Years;

To provide and maintain a Navy;

To make Rules for the Government and Regulation of the land and naval Forces;

To provide for calling forth the Militia to execute the Laws of the Union, suppress Insurrections and repel Invasions;

To provide for organizing, arming, and disciplining, the Militia, and for governing such Part of them as may be employed in the Service of the United States, reserving to the States respectively, the Appointment of the Officers, and the Authority of training the Militia according to the discipline prescribed by Congress;

To exercise exclusive Legislation in all Cases whatsoever, over such District (not exceeding ten Miles square) as may, by Cession of particular States, and the Acceptance of Congress, become the Seat of the Government of the United States, and to exercise like Authority over all Places purchased by the Consent of the Legislature of the State in which the Same shall be, for the Erection of Forts, Magazines, Arsenals, dock-Yards, and other needful Buildings;—And

To make all Laws which shall be necessary and proper for carrying into Execution the foregoing Powers, and all other Powers vested by this Constitution in the Government of the United States, or in any Department or Officer thereof.

Section 9

The Migration or Importation of such Persons as any of the States now existing shall think proper to admit, shall not be prohibited by the Congress prior to the Year one thousand eight hundred and eight, but a Tax or duty may be imposed on such Importation, not exceeding ten dollars for each Person.

The Privilege of the Writ of Habeas Corpus shall not be suspended, unless when in Cases of Rebellion or Invasion the public Safety may require it.

No Bill of Attainder or ex post facto Law shall be passed.

No Capitation, or other direct, Tax shall be laid, unless in Proportion to the Census or enumeration herein before directed to be taken.

No Tax or Duty shall be laid on Articles exported from any State.

No Preference shall be given by any Regulation of Commerce or Revenue to the Ports of one State over those of another: nor shall Vessels bound to, or from, one State, be obliged to enter, clear, or pay Duties in another.

No Money shall be drawn from the Treasury, but in Consequence of Appropriations made by Law; and a regular Statement and Account of the Receipts and Expenditures of all public Money shall be published from time to time.

No Title of Nobility shall be granted by the United States: And no Person holding any Office of Profit or Trust under them, shall, without the Consent of the Congress, accept of any present, Emolument, Office, or Title, of any kind whatever, from any King, Prince, or foreign State.

Section 10

No State shall enter into any Treaty, Alliance, or Confederation; grant Letters of Marque and Reprisal; coin Money; emit Bills of Credit; make any Thing but gold and silver Coin a Tender in Payment of Debts; pass any Bill of Attainder, ex post facto Law, or Law impairing the Obligation of Contracts, or grant any Title of Nobility.

No State shall, without the Consent of the Congress, lay any Imposts or Duties on Imports or Exports, except what may be absolutely necessary for executing it's inspection Laws: and the net Produce of all Duties and Imposts, laid by any State on Imports or Exports, shall be for the Use of the Treasury of the United States; and all such Laws shall be subject to the Revision and Control of the Congress.

No State shall, without the Consent of Congress, lay any Duty of Tonnage, keep Troops, or Ships of War in time of Peace, enter into any Agreement or Compact with another State, or with a foreign Power, or engage in War, unless actually invaded, or in such imminent Danger as will not admit of delay.

Article II
Section 1
The executive Power shall be vested in a President of the United States of America. He shall hold his Office during the Term of four Years, and, together with the Vice President, chosen for the same Term, be elected, as follows

Each State shall appoint, in such Manner as the Legislature thereof may direct, a Number of Electors, equal to the whole Number of Senators and Representatives to which the State may be entitled in the Congress: but no Senator or Representative, or Person holding an Office of Trust or Profit under the United States, shall be appointed an Elector.

The Electors shall meet in their respective States, and vote by Ballot for two Persons, of whom one at least shall not be an Inhabitant of the same State with themselves. And they shall make a List of all the Persons voted for, and of the Number of Votes for each; which List they shall sign and certify, and transmit sealed to the Seat of the Government of the United States, directed to the President of the Senate. The President of the Senate shall, in the Presence of the Senate and House of Representatives, open all the Certificates, and the Votes shall then be counted. The Person having the greatest Number of Votes shall be the President, if such Number be a Majority of the whole Number of Electors appointed; and if there be more than one who have such Majority, and have an equal Number of Votes, then the House of Representatives shall immediately chuse by Ballot one of them for President; and if no Person have a Majority, then from the five highest on the List the said House shall in like Manner chuse the President. But in chusing the President, the Votes shall be taken by States, the Representation from each State having one Vote; A quorum for this Purpose shall consist of a Member or Members from two thirds of the States, and a Majority of all the States shall be necessary to a Choice. In every Case, after the Choice of the President, the Person having the greatest Number of Votes of the Electors shall be the Vice President. But if there should remain two or more who have equal Votes, the Senate shall chuse from them by Ballot the Vice President.

The Congress may determine the Time of chusing the Electors, and the Day on which they shall give their Votes; which Day shall be the same throughout the United States.

No Person except a natural born Citizen, or a Citizen of the United States, at the time of the Adoption of this Constitution, shall be eligible to the Office of President; neither shall any Person be eligible to that Office who shall not have attained to the Age of thirty five Years, and been fourteen Years a Resident within the United States.

In Case of the Removal of the President from Office, or of his Death, Resignation, or Inability to discharge the Powers and Duties of the said Office, the Same shall devolve on the Vice President, and the Congress may by Law provide for the Case of Removal, Death, Resignation or Inability, both of the President and Vice President, declaring what Officer shall then act as President, and such Officer shall act accordingly, until the Disability be removed, or a President shall be elected.

The President shall, at stated Times, receive for his Services, a Compensation, which shall neither be increased nor diminished during the Period for which he shall have been elected, and he shall not receive within that Period any other Emolument from the United States, or any of them.

Before he enter on the Execution of his Office, he shall take the following Oath or Affirmation: —"I do solemnly swear (or affirm) that I will faithfully execute the Office of President of the United States, and will to the best of my Ability, preserve, protect and defend the Constitution of the United States."
Section 2
The President shall be Commander in Chief of the Army and Navy of the United States, and of the Militia of the several States, when called into the actual Service of the United States; he may require the Opinion, in writing, of the principal Officer in each of the executive Departments, upon any Subject relating to the Duties of their respective Offices, and he shall have Power to grant Reprieves and Pardons for Offences against the United States, except in Cases of Impeachment.

He shall have Power, by and with the Advice and Consent of the Senate, to make Treaties, provided two thirds of the Senators present concur; and he shall nominate, and by and with the Advice and Consent of the Senate, shall appoint Ambassadors, other public Ministers and Consuls, Judges of the supreme Court, and all other Officers of the United States, whose Appointments are not herein otherwise provided for, and which shall be established by Law: but the Congress may by Law vest the Appointment of such inferior Officers, as they think proper, in the President alone, in the Courts of Law, or in the Heads of Departments.

The President shall have Power to fill up all Vacancies that may happen during the Recess of the Senate, by granting Commissions which shall expire at the End of their next Session.

Section 3

He shall from time to time give to the Congress Information of the State of the Union, and recommend to their Consideration such Measures as he shall judge necessary and expedient; he may, on extraordinary Occasions, convene both Houses, or either of them, and in Case of Disagreement between them, with Respect to the Time of Adjournment, he may adjourn them to such Time as he shall think proper; he shall receive Ambassadors and other public Ministers; he shall take Care that the Laws be faithfully executed, and shall Commission all the Officers of the United States.

Section 4

The President, Vice President and all civil Officers of the United States, shall be removed from Office on Impeachment for, and Conviction of, Treason, Bribery, or other high Crimes and Misdemeanors.

Article III.

Section 1

The judicial Power of the United States, shall be vested in one supreme Court, and in such inferior Courts as the Congress may from time to time ordain and establish. The Judges, both of the supreme and inferior Courts, shall hold their Offices during good Behaviour, and shall, at stated Times, receive for their Services, a Compensation, which shall not be diminished during their Continuance in Office.

Section 2

The judicial Power shall extend to all Cases, in Law and Equity, arising under this Constitution, the Laws of the United States, and Treaties made, or which shall be made, under their Authority;—to all Cases affecting Ambassadors, other public Ministers and Consuls;—to all Cases of admiralty and maritime Jurisdiction;—to Controversies to which the United States shall be a Party;—to Controversies between two or more States;— between a State and Citizens of another State,—between Citizens of different States,—between Citizens of the same State claiming Lands under Grants of different States, and between a State, or the Citizens thereof, and foreign States, Citizens or Subjects.

In all Cases affecting Ambassadors, other public Ministers and Consuls, and those in which a State shall be Party, the supreme Court shall have original Jurisdiction. In all the other Cases before mentioned, the supreme Court shall have appellate Jurisdiction, both as to Law and Fact, with such Exceptions, and under such Regulations as the Congress shall make.

The Trial of all Crimes, except in Cases of Impeachment, shall be by Jury; and such Trial shall be held in the State where the said Crimes shall have been committed; but when not committed within any State, the Trial shall be at such Place or Places as the Congress may by Law have directed.

Section 3

Treason against the United States, shall consist only in levying War against them, or in adhering to their Enemies, giving them Aid and Comfort. No Person shall be convicted of Treason unless on the Testimony of two Witnesses to the same overt Act, or on Confession in open Court.

The Congress shall have Power to declare the Punishment of Treason, but no Attainder of Treason shall work Corruption of Blood, or Forfeiture except during the Life of the Person attainted.

Article IV

Section 1

Full Faith and Credit shall be given in each State to the public Acts, Records, and judicial Proceedings of every other State. And the Congress may by general Laws prescribe the Manner in which such Acts, Records and Proceedings shall be proved, and the Effect thereof.

Section 2

The Citizens of each State shall be entitled to all Privileges and Immunities of Citizens in the several States.

A Person charged in any State with Treason, Felony, or other Crime, who shall flee from Justice, and be found in another State, shall on Demand of the executive Authority of the State from which he fled, be delivered up, to be removed to the State having Jurisdiction of the Crime.

No Person held to Service or Labour in one State, under the Laws thereof, escaping into another, shall, in Consequence of any Law or Regulation therein, be discharged from such Service or Labour, but shall be delivered up on Claim of the Party to whom such Service or Labour may be due.

Section 3

New States may be admitted by the Congress into this Union; but no new State shall be formed or erected within the Jurisdiction of any other State; nor any State be formed by the Junction of two or more States, or Parts of States, without the Consent of the Legislatures of the States concerned as well as of the Congress.

The Congress shall have Power to dispose of and make all needful Rules and Regulations respecting the Territory or other Property belonging to the United States; and nothing in this Constitution shall be so construed as to Prejudice any Claims of the United States, or of any particular State.

Section 4

The United States shall guarantee to every State in this Union a Republican Form of Government, and shall protect each of them against Invasion; and on Application of the Legislature, or of the Executive (when the Legislature cannot be convened), against domestic Violence.

Article V

The Congress, whenever two thirds of both Houses shall deem it necessary, shall propose Amendments to this Constitution, or, on the Application of the Legislatures of two thirds of the several States, shall call a Convention for proposing Amendments, which, in either Case, shall be valid to all Intents and Purposes, as Part of this Constitution, when ratified by the Legislatures of three fourths of the several States, or by Conventions in three fourths thereof, as the one or the other Mode of Ratification may be proposed by the Congress; Provided that no Amendment which may be made prior to the Year One thousand eight hundred and eight shall in any Manner affect the first and fourth Clauses in the Ninth Section of the first Article; and that no State, without its Consent, shall be deprived of its equal Suffrage in the Senate.

Article VI

All Debts contracted, and Engagements entered into, before the Adoption of this Constitution, shall be as valid against the United States under this Constitution, as under the Confederation.

This Constitution, and the Laws of the United States which shall be made in Pursuance thereof; and all Treaties made, or which shall be made, under the Authority of the United States, shall be the supreme Law of the Land; and the Judges in every State shall be bound thereby, any Thing in the Constitution or Laws of any State to the Contrary notwithstanding.

The Senators and Representatives before mentioned, and the Members of the several State Legislatures, and all executive and judicial Officers, both of the United States and of the several States, shall be bound by Oath or Affirmation, to support this Constitution; but no religious Test shall ever be required as a Qualification to any Office or public Trust under the United States.

Article VII

The Ratification of the Conventions of nine States, shall be sufficient for the Establishment of this Constitution between the States so ratifying the Same.

The Word, "the," being interlined between the seventh and eighth Lines of the first Page, The Word "Thirty" being partly written on an Erazure in the fifteenth Line of the first Page, The Words "is tried" being interlined between the thirty second and thirty third Lines of the first Page and the Word "the" being interlined between the forty third and forty fourth Lines of the second Page.

Attest William Jackson Secretary

done in Convention by the Unanimous Consent of the States present the Seventeenth Day of September in the Year of our Lord one thousand seven hundred and Eighty seven and of the Independence of the United States of America the Twelfth In witness whereof We have hereunto subscribed our Names,

G°.Washington *Presidt and deputy from Virginia*

Delaware	South Carolina	Connecticut
Geo: Read	J. Rutledge	Wm. Saml. Johnson
Gunning Bedford jun	Charles Cotesworth	Roger Sherman
John Dickinson	Pinckney	
Richard Bassett	Charles Pinckney	**New York**
Jaco: Broom	Pierce Butler	Alexander Hamilton
Maryland	**Georgia**	**New Jersey**
James McHenry	William Few	Wil: Livingston
Dan of St Thos. Jenifer	Abr Baldwin	David Brearley
Danl. Carroll		Wm. Paterson
	New Hampshire	Jona: Dayton
Virginia	John Langdon	
John Blair	Nicholas Gilman	**Pensylvania**
James Madison Jr.		B Franklin
	Massachusetts	Thomas Mifflin
North Carolina	Nathaniel Gorham	Robt. Morris
Wm. Blount	Rufus King	Geo. Clymer
Richd. Dobbs Spaight		Thos. FitzSimons
Hu Williamson		Jared Ingersoll
		James Wilson
		Gouv Morris

Quiz

1. The Constitution of the United States sparked freedom in the minds of Americans. By 1899, how many patents had been registered with the government?
   a. Just under 50,000
   b. Just over 100,000
   c. Under 500,000
   d. Well over 600,000
2. "We hold these truths to be self-evident, that all men are created equal, that they are endowed by their Creator with certain unalienable Rights..." This comes from what American document?
   a. The Declaration of Independence
   b. The Constitution of the United States
   c. The Articles of Confederation
   d. The Federalist Papers
3. Who is credited with writing the Declaration of Independence?
   a. Ben Franklin
   b. James Madison
   c. Thomas Jefferson
   d. George Washington
4. During the early beginnings of our nation which of the following were taught in schools?
   a. The Holy Bible
   b. The Constitution of the United States
   c. The Declaration of Independence
   d. All the above
5. Who fired the "shot that was heard around the world"?
   a. The British
   b. The American Colonies
   c. Samuel Adams
   d. No one knows
6. How many men from the 13 states signed the Declaration of Independence?
   a. 13 men
   b. 39 men
   c. 42 men
   d. 56 men
7. How many references to God are mentioned in the Declaration of Independence?
   a. 2
   b. 4
   c. 6
   d. 8
8. The Declaration of Independence says: "...That to secure these rights, Governments are instituted among Men, deriving their just powers _____________..."
   a. from God
   b. from the government
   c. from the consent of the governed
   d. from the President
9. What day do we celebrate the signing of the Declaration of Independence?
   a. Memorial Day
   b. July 4th
   c. Labor Day
   d. Thanksgiving Day
10. Referencing the Declaration of Independence, "And for the support of this Declaration, with a firm reliance on the protection _________, we mutually pledge to each other our Lives, our Fortunes, and our sacred Honor."
    a. of the United States Military

    b.   of divine Providence
    c.   from the King of England
    d.   of our government

11. The following states signed the Declaration of Independence: Georgia; North Carolina; South Carolina; Massachusetts; Maryland; Virginia; Pennsylvania; Delaware; New York; New Jersey; Connecticut; __________; __________;
    a.   Maine; Vermont
    b.   Florida; West Virginia
    c.   Vermont; Tennessee
    d.   New Hampshire; Rhode Island

12. George Washington and Alexander Hamilton both signed the Declaration of Independence.
    a.   True – Both signed it
    b.   False – Neither signed it
    c.   Just George Washington signed it
    d.   Just Alexander Hamilton signed it

13. In the Constitution "We the People of the United States, in Order to form a more perfect __________,"
    a.   Country
    b.   Nation
    c.   Union
    d.   Government

14. In the Constitution of the United States, Article I pertains to:
    a.   The President's limited powers
    b.   The Congress' limited powers
    c.   The Judiciary's limited powers
    d.   Proposing and passing amendments to the Constitution

15. In the Constitution of the United States, Article II pertains to:
    a.   The President's limited powers
    b.   The Congress' limited powers
    c.   The Judiciary's limited powers
    d.   Proposing and passing amendments to the Constitution

16. In the Constitution of the United States, Article III pertains to:
    a.   The President's limited powers
    b.   The Congress' limited powers
    c.   The Judiciary's limited powers
    d.   Proposing and passing amendments to the Constitution

17. In the Constitution of the United States, Article V pertains to:
    a.   The President's limited powers
    b.   The Congress' limited powers
    c.   The Judiciary's limited powers
    d.   Proposing and passing amendments to the Constitution

18. How many men signed the Constitution of the United States?
    a.   13
    b.   39
    c.   42
    d.   56

19. How many men signed both the Declaration of Independence and the Constitution of the United States?
    a.   6
    b.   9
    c.   13
    d.   21

20. What year was the Constitution of the United States signed by the Continental Congress?
    a.   1779
    b.   1787
    c.   1789
    d.   1792

21. How many Articles and how many Amendments are currently on the Constitution of the United States?
    a.   5 Articles and 12 Amendments
    b.   7 Articles and 12 Amendments
    c.   7 Articles and 27 Amendments
    d.   9 Articles and 27 Amendments
22. Who or what determines how many Supreme Court Justices sit on the Bench?
    a.   The Constitution of the United States
    b.   The President
    c.   Congress
    d.   Declaration of Independence
23. According to the Constitution which branch of government has "All Legislative Powers" to make laws?
    a.   The President
    b.   The Congress
    c.   The Supreme Court
    d.   The Administrative Branch
24. How many years does each House of Congress serve per term?
    a.   The House serves 2 years, and the Senate serves 4 years
    b.   The House serves 4 years, and the Senate serves 6 years
    c.   The House serves 2 years, and the Senate serves 6 years
    d.   The House serves 4 years, and the Senate serves 4 years
25. How many House of Representatives and how many Senators are in Washington, D.C.?
    a.   200 House of Representatives and 100 Senators
    b.   400 House of Representatives and 200 Senators
    c.   355 House of Representatives and 200 Senators
    d.   435 House of Representatives and 100 Senators
26. Who is the President of the Senate according to the Constitution of the United States?
    a.   The Speaker of the House
    b.   The Senate Majority Leader
    c.   The President of the United States
    d.   The Vice President of the United States
27. According to the Constitution "All bills for raising revenue shall originate in the _____?"
    a.   The House of Representatives
    b.   The Senate
    c.   Executive Branch
    d.   Judicial Branch
28. According to the Constitution, how does a state determine how many electoral votes allowed for the presidential election?
    a.   Determined by the number of registered voters
    b.   Determined by the population of the state
    c.   Determined by the number of Senators and House of Representatives in Congress
    d.   Determined by the size of the state
29. Should the President become unable to serve for a period of time, the Vice President will take on the duties of the President. Who is next in line for the President should the vice president become unable to serve?
    a.   The Secretary of State
    b.   Chief of Staff
    c.   The Secretary of Defense
    d.   Speaker of the House of Representatives
30. The Supreme Court Justices are appointed by the President and serve a term of:
    a.   4 years but not more than 2 terms
    b.   6 years but not more than 2 terms
    c.   2 years but not more than 4 terms
    d.   Life-based on good behavior
31. The Supreme Court Justices are to make their decisions based on the following criteria:

    a.   Their personal interpretation of the Constitution
    b.   The Constitution is a living breathing document that changes with time
    c.   The original intent of the Constitution
    d.   Based on political expediency

32. A proposed amendment may be sent to the states for ratification when:
    a.   51% of the House of Representatives and the Senate pass it, and the President signs it
    b.   Two-thirds of the House of Representatives and Senate pass it
    c.   When two-thirds of the state's legislative convention pass it
    d.   Either answer b or c

33. Before an amendment becomes a law, ___________ must ratify the amendment.
    a.   Three-quarters of the state's legislative convention
    b.   51% of the state's legislative convention
    c.   Three-quarters of the state governors
    d.   The President of the United States

34. Which of the following two Founders did not sign the Constitution of the United States
    a.   George Washington and Roger Sherman
    b.   Thomas Jefferson and Samuel Adams
    c.   Ben Franklin and James Wilson
    d.   Alexander Hamilton and George Read

35. Which of the original 13 states was not present during the signing of the Constitution?
    a.   Maryland
    b.   New Hampshire
    c.   Rhode Island
    d.   Georgia

36. How many Bill of Rights were originally sent to the states for ratification?
    a.   8
    b.   10
    c.   12
    d.   14

37. Which amendment speaks of "The separation of church and state"?
    a.   The first amendment
    b.   The second amendment
    c.   The fourth amendment
    d.   There is nothing in the Constitution that speaks of a separation of church and state

38. The second amendment guarantees our right to "...keep and bear Arms," which means:
    a.   The people may own pistols
    b.   The people may own rifles
    c.   The people may own as many guns as they choose
    d.   All the above

39. The powers not delegated to the United States by the Constitution, nor prohibited by it to the States, are reserved to the States respectively, or to the people.
    a.   This is the sixth amendment
    b.   This is the seventh amendment
    c.   This is the tenth amendment
    d.   This is the twelfth amendment

40. Which amendment made slavery unconstitutional?
    a.   The thirteenth amendment
    b.   The fourteenth amendment
    c.   The eighteenth amendment
    d.   The twentieth amendment

41. Which amendment allowed all citizens of the United States to vote regardless of race?
    a.   The thirteenth amendment
    b.   The fifteenth amendment
    c.   The seventeenth amendment
    d.   The twentieth amendment

42. Which amendment gave Congress the ability to charge the American People taxes on our income in the year 1913?

    a.   The sixteenth amendment
    b.   The eighteenth amendment
    c.   The twentieth amendment
    d.   The twenty-fifth amendment

43. Which amendment took over 202 years to be ratified by the states?
    a.   The eleventh amendment
    b.   The fifteenth amendment
    c.   The twentieth amendment
    d.   The twenty-seventh amendment

44. Who called the Federalist Papers: "the best commentary on the principles of government, which ever was written"?
    a.   Ben Franklin
    b.   George Washington
    c.   Thomas Jefferson
    d.   Samuel Adams

45. Which of the Founders were not involved in the writings of the Federalist Papers?
    a.   Alexander Hamilton
    b.   John Jay
    c.   James Madison
    d.   John Adams

46. Forbid it, Almighty God! I know not what course others may take; but as for me, give me liberty or give me death.
    a.   Ben Franklin said this
    b.   James Monroe said this
    c.   Patrick Henry said this
    d.   George Washington said this

47. Providence has given to our people the choice of their rulers, and it is the duty, as well as the privilege and interest of our Christian nation to select and prefer Christians for their rulers.
    a.   Quote by Chief Justice of the Supreme Court John Jay
    b.   Quote by President George Washington
    c.   Quote by Secretary of State Edmund Jennings Randolph
    d.   Quote by U.S. Senator George Read

48. Who declared that "religion is deemed in other countries incompatible with good government and yet proved by our experience to be its best support?"
    a.   Alexander Hamilton
    b.   John Hancock
    c.   Thomas Jefferson
    d.   Ben Franklin

49. Who is quoted as saying: Where, say some, is the king of America? I'll tell you, friend, He reigns above.
    a.   Thomas Paine
    b.   William Paterson
    c.   George Mason
    d.   Roger Sherman

50. Which Founder said: "I have alternately been called an Aristocrat and a Democrat. I am neither. I am a Christocrat."
    a.   Benjamin Rush
    b.   Ben Franklin
    c.   Thomas Jefferson
    d.   George Read

Answers to the Quiz:

1. d	11. d	21. c	31. c	41. b
2. a	12. b	22. c	32. d	42. a
3. c	13. c	23. b	33. a	43. d
4. d	14. b	24. c	34. b	44. c
5. d	15. a	25. d	35. c	45. d
6. d	16. c	26. d	36. c	46. c
7. b	17. d	27. a	37. d	47. a
8. c	18. b	28. c	38. d	48. c
9. b	19. a	29. d	39. c	49. a
10. b	20. b	30. d	40. a	50. a

What's Next

Please look for more information on my website – God, Country and Family at www.ardentcopy.org

Here is a list of the E-Books that will be available soon on the site:
- 50 States – One Nation under God
- 1st Amendment – What's the significance of…
- 2nd Amendment – Why we can't live without it
- The Power of Article V
- How Communism was introduced into Congress
- How the Administrative State affects our lives
- The power of the 10th Amendment

And much more…

Bibliography

Skousen, W. C. (2009). *The Five Thousand Year Leap: 28 great ideas that changed the world*. Franklin, TN: American Documents Publishing, L.L.C.

Spalding, M., & Forte, D. F. (2014). *The Heritage guide to the Constitution*. Washington, DC: Regnery Publishing.

Hamilton, Alexander; Madison, James; and Jay, John. *The Federalist Papers*. New York: Penguin Group (USA) Inc., 1961

Ralph Ketcham. *The Anti-Federalist Papers and the Constitutional Convention Debates*. New York: New American Library, 1986

Barton, D. (2013). *Original Intent: the Courts, the Constitution, and Religion*. Cork: BookBaby.

The U.S. Constitution: a reader. (2012). Hillsdale, MI: Hillsdale College Press.

West, T. G. (2001). *Vindicating the founders: race, sex, class, and justice in the origins of America*. Lanham, MD: Rowman & Littlefield .

Webster, Noah. *Noah Webster's 1828 Dictionary*. Chesapeake: Foundation for American Christian Education, 1995. Print.

Federer, William J. *America's God and Country Encyclopedia of Quotations*. Coppell: Fame Publishing, Inc., 1994. Print.

Tocqueville, A. D., Mansfield, H. C., & Winthrop, D. (2000). Democracy in America. doi:10.7208/chicago/9780226924564.001.0001

DSouza, D. (2018). *Death of a Nation*. St. Martins Press.